Leah C. Adams

HEBREWS
A BETTER BLEND

AN EIGHT-WEEK BIBLE STUDY

Published by Warner Press Inc
Warner Press and "WP" logo are trademarks of Warner Press Inc

HeBrews: A Better Blend
Written by Leah Adams

Tree 1:3, an imprint of Warner Press, publishes ministry resources designed to help people grow more deeply in their faith.

Requests for information should be sent to:
Warner Press Inc
1201 East Fifth Street
P.O. Box 2499
Anderson, IN 46012
www.warnerpress.org

Editors: Karen Rhodes, Robin Fogle
Cover by Christian Elden
Design and layout by Curtis Corzine

All photos copyright ©Thinkstock and their rightful owners

ISBN: 978-1-59317-737-9

Printed in the USA

ENDORSEMENTS

Prepare to be changed when you drink deeply from HeBrews: A Better Blend, the newest Bible study by Leah Adams. Her study challenges us to dig into Scriptures—and into our very own souls—by applying ancient words to our contemporary lives. Leah peels back the pages of Hebrews in a way that makes us thirsty—thirsty to go deeper and deeper—straight into the heart of Christ. I met Jesus again and again in these pages.

Jennifer Dukes Lee
author of the forthcoming book *Love Idol* (Tyndale Momentum) www.jenniferdukeslee.com

The book of Hebrews teaches us so much about the amazing character of Christ. Always personal and with soul-fulfilling significance for our generation, no one teaches the Bible quite like Leah Adams. Leah's modern and personal look at the book of Hebrews offers a look at love, legacy, and faith in a God who never fails.

Brooke Keith

Author of *Chrissie's Shell, Notes from God for a Woman's Heart, Forever His: Encouragement for Young Women,* and *Radically Red* (Warner Press) www.laurabrookekeith.wordpress.com

Sometimes, for me, stepping into the study of God's Word is like stepping into a Bath and Body Works™ Store. Yep—it all smells so YUMMY I want it all at once. In a Bath and Body Works™, I am utterly dependent upon a knowledgeable and passionate sales person to help me focus and actually walk away with something I enjoy. As silly as the analogy may be, that is what came to my mind as I was trying to wrap words around this great study that Leah has written. To me, the Bible is so full of life-changing fragrance I sometimes have no idea where to start. In this study of Hebrews, Leah accomplishes the great task of helping us navigate these amazing fragrances (is that coffee I smell?) in the form of truth, and helps us FOCUS on the priceless takeaway of its treasure. Through these pages Leah will take every reader into a "set-apart" place that draws out a sweet aroma and a rich blend from God's Word that will leave you better than you were when you started. That is my goal for any study I undertake.

Mission accomplished, Leah!

Pat Layton
Author and Speaker, www.patlayton.net

Leah Adams lives the words that she writes. She doesn't waste words; instead, she lavishly invests them into the hearts of those who sit beneath her influence. In her second Bible study release, HeBrews: A Better Blend, Leah continues to weave a legacy of faith by challenging readers to come alongside her and to dig deeply in and around, beneath and beyond, the rich words of faith penned in the book of Hebrews. Leah's depth of insight into God's Word is equally matched by her ability to lead others to a similar understanding. Her pilgrimage of faith is a fervent pursuit of the Father. Those who choose to make this journey with Leah will cross paths with Jesus Christ along the way and be duly challenged to keep in step with His transforming grace.

F. Elaine Olsen
Christian Author and Speaker, www.peaceforthejourney.com

CONTENTS

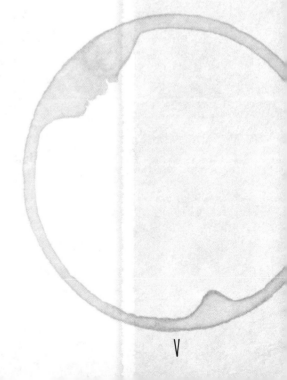

ACKNOWLEDGMENTS

When I began writing this Bible study, I had no intention of publishing it. I self-published my first Bible study, *From the Trash Pile to the Treasure Chest: Creating a Godly Legacy*, and while that was mostly a good experience, I knew I probably would not go down that path again.

A reasonable question at this point might be the following: "So, Leah, why did you even bother to write a Bible study on Hebrews if you had no intention of publishing it?"

To be totally honest, I asked myself the same question multiple times throughout the writing. The only conclusion I could come to was that I was simply being obedient to do what God required. I knew that Hebrews and faith were my topics, and I desired to be obedient to what God asked. So, I wrote.

About halfway into this huge undertaking I was introduced to Karen Rhodes at Warner Press. My dear friend, Brooke Keith, had authored a book and some other pieces for Warner and she encouraged Karen to read some of my blog posts. The rest is history and here I am working on my third project with Karen and the wonderful folks at Warner Press. I am grateful for Karen's wisdom and guidance as I journeyed down this path. Her vast knowledge of the industry has taught me some valuable lessons, and I know this manuscript is much better because of Karen.

I have two friends who have been used by the Lord to cheer me on as I wrote. Elaine Olsen has been a wonderful source of encouragement and support as I have ridden the roller coaster of writing this study. She has urged me on and reminded me many times that we write because we desire to glorify Jesus, and Him alone. Elaine, you are a precious sister in Christ. Candy Bradley, a retired educator, put in countless hours reviewing the manuscript for grammar and punctuation errors. In addition, Candy, who knows me fairly well, was willing to tell me when portions of the manuscript were not working and needed to be changed. I am so grateful for her willingness to speak truth to me, even at the risk of our friendship. Thank you, Candy.

There are many people who cover me in prayer on a regular basis, but none more faithfully than Zelda Merritt. In spite of battling significant health problems in the past few years, Zelda covers my ministry and writing in prayer. Every month she faithfully sends me a hand-made card, reminding me of her prayers for me. Thank you, Zelda.

I believe family members of an author walk where angels fear to tread. A good writing day can produce a good outlook and a happy wife, while a writing day full of frustrations and interruptions can unveil moods and attitudes in an author that are not pretty. My husband, Greg, has seen both ends of that spectrum, and I am grateful that he loves me in spite of it.

Finally, to my Jesus…the Audience of One. I write because of Him and to please Him. It amazes me that He entrusts such an important kingdom agenda item to me, the prodigal son's sister. He empowers me to write and encourages me to persevere through His indwelling Holy Spirit. I pray His Words are what you read in the pages that follow. Thank You, Jesus, for offering Yourself in payment for my sin. I love You! I worship You! I honor You with this gift of words.

Note to the Reader:

Those of us who have studied the Bible in an effort to grow in our faith know that there are many different commentaries and reference books available. The authors of these books may differ greatly at times in their interpretation of the Scriptures, based on their scholarly studies and their denominational backgrounds.

We, at Warner Press, strive to keep our Bible studies theologically sound and doctrinally unbiased; however, we also want to give our authors the freedom to share their beliefs and convictions. We recognize that not everyone will hold the same views, but differing opinions can be used by God to challenge us to grow.

Our hope and prayer is that as you study the Bible, you will use our Bible studies as a guide to deeper understanding. Evaluate the material presented, ask questions, and pursue answers, knowing that many interpretations exist. Allow God to speak His truth into your life personally, as you seek to apply the knowledge you gain. May the Holy Spirit use this Bible study time to teach you the important lessons He has for you. May you be filled with His grace and know the depths of His love.

The Editors

HeBrews: A Better Blend

**The new is in the old concealed; the old is by the new revealed.
—St. Augustine**

Hello! And welcome to the second Bible study in the Legacy series. The first study was entitled *From the Trash Pile to the Treasure Chest: Creating a Godly Legacy*, and it examined three key aspects of a godly legacy: faith, character and holiness. The study you have before you is a study of the book of Hebrews, the *pièce de résistance* in the Word of God, on the topic of faith. I am calling it *HeBrews: A Better Blend*, because the book of Hebrews is all about better things, with faith in Jesus being the centering point for all things better. In addition to Hebrews being about better things, the writer of Hebrews blended a beautiful mixture of Old Covenant theology with Jesus and the New Covenant He instituted with His blood.

I thought it would be fun to go with a coffee and dessert theme for the study since coffee and Bible study go together like peanut butter and jelly, biscuits and gravy, Romeo and Juliet, Democrats and Republicans. Well, perhaps that last one was not a good analogy. I imagine that coffee and dessert are part of many Bible study group meetings, so both will definitely play a part in our study of Hebrews. In fact, you will find recipes for yummy desserts at the beginning of each chapter. I have enlisted the help of family and friends, as well as a foraging into my own recipe files to offer you the yummiest selection of dessert treats. I encourage you to try them with your Bible study group or make them for your own personal enjoyment.

Very few books of the Bible lend themselves to a compare and contrast method of study, but Hebrews allows us to study in this way. Throughout the course of the study we will be looking at all sorts of better things, and in doing so our study will take us deep into the Old Testament. Please don't let that frighten you. The Old Testament is chock-full of tiramisu-rich stories that find their completion in the New Testament. As we look at a concept in the Old Testament we will have the opportunity to read "the rest of the story," as Paul Harvey said, from the New Testament. The completed story, the better things, and real life application are what we are pursuing in this study.

I feel as if I owe you a bit of a disclaimer right about now, so here it is: Hebrews is not a simple book to study, nor is it an easy read. There are challenging passages that will require the exercise of no small amount of brain cells. Some passages may even provoke a bit of friendly disagreement. Old Testament passages, or references to Old Testament passages, show up frequently.

It is not clear who authored Hebrews, nor is the identity of the intended audience clearly spelled out. In this study you will learn why Jesus and the salvation He offers is better than that offered to the Hebrews of antiquity through the Old Covenant. Your heart will be tender as you consider Who Jesus was and the great sacrifice He made for you. You will be encouraged by the faith journeys of regular men and women we consider to be heroes of the faith. Along the way I hope you will find encouragement to walk out your own faith journey in a more committed way because of Who Jesus is and what He has done for you. Our study of Hebrews may not be easy, but it will bring forth beautiful results as you faithfully apply it to your heart and life.

As we journey through Hebrews, examining what the Word has to teach us, we will move swiftly through some chapters, but will camp out for a time in others. Please understand I am not saying that certain chapters of Hebrews are more important than others. I simply want us to be able to narrow our focus and zero in on key concepts in this wonderful book, and to do that we must move more quickly through certain passages.

So, pour yourself a steaming cup of coffee (or tea, if perchance you are not a coffee drinker), help yourself to a warm slice of coffeecake, and let's get started. It is my distinct pleasure to welcome you to *HeBrews: A Better Blend*.

Leah

MAY I SERVE YOU?

I thought we would start our time together this week with my husband's favorite cake recipe…a cream cheese pound cake. This is a timeless recipe that has been around for decades and probably appears in every church cookbook that has ever been offered by church ladies. It is simple to make with only six ingredients, yet tastes incredibly rich and wonderful. If you are looking for the perfect drink to pair with this wonderfully rich, dense, pound cake, I'm going to suggest a tall glass of cold milk. I'm pretty sure God would bless this cake for dessert, for a snack, or for breakfast…or perhaps all three in the same day! Topping your piece of cake with ice cream is optional. I don't; my man does.

Brew up a cup of Green Mountain Caramel Vanilla Cream® coffee and enjoy!!

RECIPE

CREAM CHEESE POUND CAKE

1 - 8 oz. block cream cheese (no substitutes and no low fat imitations)

¾ cup (3 sticks) butter (REAL butter, not margarine)

3 cups sugar

6 eggs

3 cups cake flour

1 teaspoonful vanilla

Cream together butter, cream cheese and sugar until they are light and fluffy. Add eggs one at a time, mixing well after each addition. Add flour and stir until just mixed in. Stir in vanilla. Place in greased and lightly floured tube or Bundt pan. Bake at 325° for 90 minutes. Allow cake to cool in pan for 1 hour. Turn out and serve.

WEEK 1- A BETTER NAME: JESUS – VENTI ESPRESSO

Jesus

Son of God

Savior

Redeemer

Lamb of God

Lion of Judah

Messiah

Prince of Peace

Jesus: the name that is above all other names. The first time I put the name with a face was in my childhood Sunday school room. The Jesus in the picture frame had long flowing light brown hair, smooth white skin, blue eyes, and a smile that spoke peace into my young heart. The frame was bent, the picture was faded and the room smelled more than a little musty, but the picture made the room seem holy. It wasn't until I was in my thirties (30s) that I realized the real Jesus would probably have looked quite different than my Sunday school Jesus. Jesus was Jewish, which meant he probably had darker skin, hair and eyes. The peaceful smile? Well, that is where my Sunday school Jesus and the real Jesus probably had a lot in common. Seeing the smile of Jesus is one of those things I am eagerly anticipating when I get to heaven. I'm hoping His smile will be accompanied by a "well done, good and faithful servant."

This week our Hebrews study will take us through the first four chapters of this marvelous book. The material we study this week will offer an important foundation for the rest of our study so please give it your full attention. By the time you finish day 5, you will have read the first four chapters of Hebrews and found one of my favorite verses, Hebrews 4:12. Actually I have several favorite verses in Hebrews, but 4:12 is probably the first of my favorites.

Fix your eyes on Jesus, dear one. *(That's in Hebrews 12, but it is timeless advice.)* Perhaps your Jesus and my Sunday school Jesus look a lot alike. That's okay. Go ahead and dive into Hebrews because we are going to gain a whole new visual of Jesus as we study. This entire book is about Jesus and what He did for you and me.

Day 1 – Angels? Jesus? Which is Better?

The writer of Hebrews opens the very first chapter with such a powerful description of God's work I feel breathless each time I read it. He covers Genesis to Revelation in the short span of 4 verses. It was almost as if he felt a sense of urgency to make his point before someone called "*TIME!*" Read **Hebrews 1:1-4** for yourself and see if you feel the same way.

List some words or phrases that stand out to you in these verses and explain why they are significant to you. I'll go first.

God spoke…at many times and in various ways…. – This tells me that God is infinitely patient and gloriously creative. He knew we would not *GET* the concept of Jesus and salvation the first time, but we would each need to be spoken to in unique ways in order for us to understand.

_____

_____

_____

_____

What do you think? Are those not four powerful verses that cover creation, the prophets, the gospels and the Revelation? The writer is saying that God invaded our world in the person of Jesus, and He provided the salvation the ancients longed to see. Perhaps I am getting ahead of myself here. Let me give you a bit of background to the book of Hebrews, and hopefully you will better understand why I think these four verses are so powerful.

Why would the writer of the book of Hebrews feel so compelled to cover all of history in the space of 4 verses? We can only guess that it had something to do with the fact that his readers were slowly slipping back into the ways and customs of ancient Judaism, despite the fact they had apparently received Jesus as their Lord and Savior. Although we do not know the identity of the writer of Hebrews, we can easily deduce that he or she knew the audience well and the audience trusted and looked up to him or her. From this point forward I will use the words "him" or "he" to identify the writer of Hebrews with the understanding that some scholars believe the author could have been a "she," namely Priscilla. Other scholars are firm in the belief that Paul is the author, while an equal number disagree and offer various names such as Apollos, Barnabas, Philip, Silas or Luke as the writer. Let's not allow a lack of knowledge of the identity of the

author to deter us from the real message of the book. Regardless of who penned the book of Hebrews, it is clear the ultimate author was the Holy Spirit. That, my friends, is bedrock when we think about biblical authorship.

Now let's turn to the audience. Who were they? Were they Jew or Gentile? Greek, Roman, or Jewish? Rich or poor? Old or young? Had any of them actually known Jesus or were they second generation Christians? In fact, were they Christians at all? Most scholars agree the writer of Hebrews was writing to a congregation of Jews who had come to faith in Christ at some point in the past. Perhaps some had even been alive when Jesus was crucified at the age of 33, because the writer talks about the temple (in Jerusalem) in his writings. The temple was destroyed by the Romans in A.D. 70, so obviously the audience lived within 40 years of the death of Jesus. It is reasonable to think some of them might have met Jesus.

> We will find as we move on that the audience was experiencing a waning faith in Christ because of persecution of some type and in fact, was being tempted to go back to the old practices of Judaism. Consider what Warren Wiersbe says of these Christians and the time in which they lived. "It (Hebrews) was written at a time when the ages were colliding and when everything in society seemed to be shaking. It was written to Christians who were wondering what was going on and what they could do about it. The stability of the old was passing away, and their faith was wavering." [1]

Sound familiar? This could easily be describing the day in which you and I live, couldn't it? I'm praying you and I will find courage in the pages of Hebrews to press on and press into Jesus as we live in this shaking, colliding world.

For all we do not know about the writer and audience of the book of Hebrews, I believe we can agree with the following from Word Biblical Commentary.

> "Hebrews is a sermon rooted in actual life. It is addressed to a local gathering of men and women who discovered that they could be penetrated by adverse circumstances over which they exercised no control." [2]

Perhaps Hebrews is more applicable to our lives today than we might think.

Are there adverse circumstances in your life over which you exercise no control? Note them here.

_____

_____

_____

_____

How could **Hebrews 1:1-4** encourage you in the circumstances you just listed?

_____

_____

_____

_____

Let's review what we know thus far.

1. Hebrews is probably a sermon written for a group of Christian Jews in the years following the crucifixion of Jesus.

2. These Jews were experiencing, or had experienced, persecution for their faith.

3. They were tempted to go back to the old ways of Judaism, which was a works-based system of sacrifices and practices.

4. The writer of Hebrews, in a blazing burst of words, attempts to remind them of their history with God and all He has done for them in sending Jesus to die for their sin.

5. God was establishing that Jesus was His Son in these opening verses. He was establishing the Christology of Jesus.

If I had to offer you one sentence that would summarize the book of Hebrews it would be this: *Jesus is better than anything or anyone.*

Hebrews 1 is all about the God-ness of Jesus. In these verses, God, through the pen of the writer, is telling us something very important. I love the way my friend Kathie puts it. Consider her words: "We can say to any soul who is curious about God: read, study, watch, look at JESUS. The One you see Him to be in scripture is Who you can trust the Father to be. If you want to know how the Father thinks

and feels about you, look at JESUS. See how JESUS spoke to people, see what He did and we can know for sure, for sure, what God the Father is like!! There is no need, no excuse, for any soul to be ignorant about Who God is. The Bible tells us!"[3]

The writer of Hebrews used this sermon in an attempt to convince the readers of Jesus' supremacy over the old ways of Judaism, as well as over angels, Moses, and the Old Covenant. We will see this in glorious display as we go through this study because it is all about the better things Jesus offers. The writer dives right into this discussion of better things by taking his congregation into a discussion of angels. Let's listen in.

Please read **Hebrews 1:4-14** and note here every reference to angels. Be sure to include the sentence and verse in which it is found.

_____

_____

_____

_____

As soon as the author of Hebrews takes a breath from verses 1-4, he launches into the first discourse about Jesus being better than angels.

Angels? Where did that come from?

More background. Because angels figured so prominently in the Old Testament, many Jews exalted angels to a high place. Some of them believed the Old Covenant was given to Moses by angels. Other Jews believed that God had a "congress" of angels whose purpose was to provide advice and guidance to Him. As you can see, these false beliefs went a long way toward causing an almost god-like persona to be assigned to angels. In fact, Gnosticism allowed angels to be worshiped and reduced Jesus to an angel. In short and without going into a whole study on angels, the writer of Hebrews knew that this topic of Jesus' status as compared with angels _must_ be addressed.

Consider again **Hebrews 1:5-14** and answer the following questions:

What is Jesus called twice in verse 5?

_____

_____

Consider an interesting thought from John MacArthur: "Son is an incarnational title of Christ. Though His son ship was anticipated in the Old Testament (Proverbs 30:4), He did not receive the title of Son until He was begotten into time. Prior to time and His incarnation he was eternal God with God. The term Son has only to do with Jesus Christ in His incarnation. It is only an analogy to say that God is Father, and Jesus is Son—God's way of helping us understand the essential relationship between the first and second Persons of the Trinity." [4]

Do you agree with MacArthur? What are your thoughts about this quote? There are no right or wrong answers, but be sure to discuss this with your Bible study group.

_____

_____

What are the angels commanded to do in verse 6?

_____

_____

In verse 8, the writer uses a passage from Psalm 45 to proclaim the deity of Jesus. In addition to Son what other name is Jesus called in verse 8?

_____

_____

By utilizing a passage in verses 10-12 from Psalm 102:25-27, the writer of Hebrews establishes Jesus as taking part in what major event that we read about in Genesis 1?

_____

_____

Jesus is BETTER than the angels. The writer of Hebrews is beginning his orchestration of the Christology of Jesus. He wants his audience to understand that Jesus is not another angel. He is the eternal Son of God who is worshiped by the angels. He was not a created being, but rather He is the Creator of the universe. He will never grow old, nor will He ever die again. In fact, He is, even now, seated in the place of honor at the right hand of God in heaven. In verse 14, the writer deals the final blow by telling his readers that angels are spirits sent to minister to those who will receive the salvation provided by Jesus. The authority of Christ was established.

Anything you and I perceive as greater than Jesus becomes an idol to us, and we are in grave danger of worshiping it. Just as the Hebrew Christians idolized angels, you and I have a propensity to idolize things or people in our culture. We worship money, children, homes, jobs, health, spouses, friends, abilities, our looks, status and so much more. Even today angel worship occurs. Jesus is better than all of these. We are wise if we keep created things in perspective. Only Jesus is the Son of God, the Creator of the Universe, the King of Kings and Lord of Lords. Only He came to die in order that you and I might have eternal salvation. Jesus is BETTER.

MEDITATION MOMENT:

What things or people tend to rise up as idols in your life? Are you willing to ask God to reveal to you any idols you may have reserved in your heart? I promise if you will ask, He will show them to you. It is only when we turn those idols over to God and allow Jesus to reign supremely on the throne of our hearts that we will find true peace and joy. Just do it!!

Day 2 – Becoming Like Us

In the summer I love to watch the hummingbirds that visit my feeders upon their return from South America. They fly around seeking delectable nectar for their food. These tiny birds are fiercely territorial, often dive-bombing another hummer who encroaches upon their feeding site. As they hover above the feeders, they perform an almost hypnotic dance, swinging back and forth until the decision is made to perch and feed. Their tiny wings that beat at amazing speeds, as well as their unique chirp, make them easily identifiable.

At least once each year, I find a hummer who has flown by accident into my large living room windows and met an unfortunate end. Occasionally, they will fly into the window and simply addle themselves. When this happens, they sit on my deck for a long while, regaining their senses, and then fly off. When I find them after their crash, I am sad and think, "Oh little hummy! If only I could speak your language and warn you about those big ol' windows. If only I could become one of you."

In the second chapter of Hebrews the writer reminds his readers that Jesus did, in fact, become one of us. He did this so He could not only warn us of the dangers of flying in Satan's territory, but also provide a way to escape Satan's clutches.

Please take time right now to read **Hebrews 2** and write here every reference or name by which Jesus is called.

_____

_____

_____

_____

As this chapter opens, the writer is saying to his readers, "Listen up! Pay attention! Remember! You have a great salvation, but you are in danger of being rebuked because of your neglect of it." He was, in effect, saying to the Jewish Christians that if they thought the penalties for not keeping the Old Testament law were bad, they better wake up, because failing to cling to their salvation would bring even worse punishment or rebuke.

After using chapter one of Hebrews to establish Jesus as the Son of God, the writer utilizes his second chapter to establish the humanity and suffering of Christ as He came to earth to provide salvation. A great question to ask at this point might be: Was the God-ness of Jesus more important than the human-ness, or was the human-ness more important than the God-ness when it comes to salvation? My answer would be, "Both were critical." Let's look to four verses in chapter two in order to sort this out.

Recall that we established Jesus' divinity in chapter one. He is God; He is the Son of God. Therefore, that means He is perfect and holy. He is completely sinless and totally righteous. Keeping that in mind, consider again **Hebrews 2:14-18** (NIV1984).

Fill in the blanks of these five verses. I have included highlights (in parentheses) I do not want you to miss:

- *Since the children (that is you and me) have flesh and blood, he (Jesus) too*
  _____ _____ *their humanity so that by his*
  _____ *he might destroy him who holds the*
  _____ *of death—that is, the devil.*

- *And free those who all their lives were held in slavery by their fear of*
  _____.

- *For surely it is not angels he _____, but Abraham's descendants (Jews and Gentiles who are willing to accept Him).*

- *For this reason he had to be _____*
  _____ *his brothers (you and me),*
  in _____ _____ in order that he might
  become a merciful and faithful high priest in service to God, and that he might
  make _____ for (pay the fine for) the sin
  (disobedience and rebellion) of the people.

- *Because he himself _____when he was*
  tempted, (remember, the God-ness of Jesus was not tempted, the humanness
  was), he is able to help those who are being _____.

In order for Jesus to pay the fine for our rebellion and disobedience to God, He had to become one of us. Jesus, as God, could not identify with temptation, but Jesus as man totally experienced temptation. The difference is that while you and I sometimes give in to temptation, Jesus never did. He overcame it by engaging the Word of God and prayer.

Our rebellion and disobedience is against God, bringing consequences and a penalty. The consequence is separation from a perfect and holy God, while the penalty is eternal death. In Jesus' final earthly act, He died on the cross to pay the penalty for our rebellion and disobedience. His death on the cross said to God, "I will pay the fine owed by mankind. You give mankind My holy standing so they do not have to be separated from Us (God the Father, God the Son, and God the Holy Spirit)."

Allow me to show you this using a few verses from outside of Hebrews. Fill in the blanks of these verses.

- **Psalm 139:1–2 (NKJV):** *O Lord, you have searched me and _____ .*

God knows you inside and out—completely.

- **Romans 3:23 (NIV1984):** *For _____ have sinned and fall short of the glory of God.*

All means you. All means me. None of us measure up to the perfection of God. No one. Our rebellion and disobedience to God's commands is sin.

- **Romans 6:23 (NIV1984):** *For the wages of sin is _____, but the _____ of God is eternal life in Christ Jesus our Lord.*

Rebellion and disobedience have consequences, and the consequences according to God are death—separation from God forever and ever.

- **Romans 5:8 (NIV1984):** *But God demonstrates His own _____ for _____ in this: While we were _____ sinners, Christ died for us.*

God loved you and me so much that He didn't want us to be separated from Him forever. Since our rebellion required a payment by death, God sent Jesus to die on the cross in your place, paying the fine that you owed for your rebellion and disobedience. He did this long before you ever realized you needed Him to be the boss, the king, and the ruler of your life.

- **Romans 10:9 (NIV1984):** *That if you confess with your mouth, Jesus is Lord, and _____ in your _____ that God raised Him from the dead, you will be saved.*

Jesus did the hard work. He died a horrible death on a cross to pay the fine you and I owed for our rebellion and disobedience. Each of us must ask Him to forgive our rebellion and disobedience and allow His death to pay the penalty for our sin.

- **Romans 10:13:** *For _____ who calls on the name of the Lord will be saved.*

Anyone who sincerely and honestly asks Jesus to come into their heart and be their best friend will find that He is faithful to do that.

- **Hebrews 7:25:** *Therefore He is able to save _____ those who come to God through Him, because He always lives to _____ for them.*

Once you ask Jesus to come into your heart and live, He will not only enable you to live a godly life; He will also go to God on your behalf, seeking His best for your life.

Have you ever asked Jesus to come into your heart and be your very best friend and the companion who never leaves you? If not, today can be the day! Right now, as you sit before Him, perhaps you recognize that you have never taken the first step of asking Him to come into your heart and change your life. If you would like to do that, I encourage you to pray this prayer or something similar:

"Dear Jesus, I realize You died on the cross to pay the debt for my sin. I know You rose from the grave to give me life forever with You in heaven, and You in my heart right here on earth. Please forgive me for my rebellion and disobedience. I ask You to come into my heart and be my forever-friend. Help me to live in a way that is pleasing to You. Thank You, Jesus, for never giving up on me. I love You. Amen.

Dear friend, if you prayed that prayer and made those words your very own, Jesus now lives in your heart, and He will never, ever leave you. Having Jesus in your heart does not mean life will always be easy. It does mean that He will be with you to guide and help you through whatever God allows in your life.

I am so proud of you. He is so proud of you and loves you so much. Tomorrow we will continue our study of how Jesus is better than anything else in your life.

MEDITATION MOMENT:

In the space provided, journal about your salvation experience. Include what brought you to the realization that you needed Jesus in your life. Who was influential in helping you get to that point? Do you remember where you were and on what date this occurred? Did someone lead you in prayer, or were you alone? How did you feel at that time? Write as much or as little as you like, but please, take time to write down the basics of your salvation experience.

Day 3 — Soften Up Toward Jesus!

When a baby is born, the arteries in her body are strong, elastic, and flexible, allowing blood to carry oxygen and nutrients from the heart to the rest of the body. By her early 20s, small amounts of plaque have begun to form in those arteries. As she ages, her arteries, affected by things like high blood pressure, diabetes, and high cholesterol, become stiff. This may prevent blood from flowing to organs and tissues that need it. This stiffening of the arteries is called arteriosclerosis. The old timers called it hardening of the arteries.

Modern medicine knows that this hardening of the arteries in the body can lead to many serious and often fatal complications, such as heart attacks and strokes. The writer of Hebrews knew a little something about this concept of hardening. In the third chapter of Hebrews, he warned his readers three times against hardening their hearts. The Greek word he used each time was *skleryno*, which means "to make hard or stiff." [5] Each time this word is used in the New Testament it is used figuratively rather than literally, and it is always used in reference to the heart or mind. Do you see the similarity in the two words: *arterioSCLERosis* and *SKLERyno*? Any time you see the root word *skler*, you can immediately know it is referring to something being hardened.

Today, as we study Hebrews chapter three, I want us to allow the Word to examine our hearts just as the writer of Hebrews urged the Jewish Christians to do. Read **Hebrews 3:1-6** and answer the following questions:

By what two names is Jesus called in verse 1?

_____

_____

The reference to Jesus as "Apostle" occurs only in this verse in Hebrews and may strike us as odd, but let's think this through for a moment. We are most familiar with the use of the word *apostle* in reference to the twelve men chosen by Jesus to walk alongside of Him in ministry.

Please explain what you believe to be the primary role of the twelve apostles.

_____

_____

_____

The English word apostle comes from the Greek word *apostolos,* and it means to send forth; envoy, ambassador, commissioned agent. Jesus intended for His apostles to go forth in His name and under His commissioning to spread the Gospel to the world. As we think about Jesus being called Apostle in Hebrews 3, we can understand this word being used by God because He sent Jesus forth, commissioned to bring salvation and restoration to all who were fallen. Jesus truly was the ultimate apostle. We will spend much time later in the study on Jesus' role as High Priest, so let's table that discussion for now.

Jews in ancient times considered Moses to be one of the greatest men who ever lived. It is possible they even considered Moses to be greater than Jesus Christ. The author of Hebrews intended to immediately address this misconception in chapter 3, just as he addressed the issue of angels in chapter one. When we begin to elevate a thing or person to a place of worship, something else has to be removed from that same pedestal. As Christians, both then and now, we must keep Jesus the sole focus of our worship. We, along with the Hebrews of antiquity, are reminded that while Moses was a faithful servant in God's house, Jesus was the one Who built the house and He deserves all our worship.

List some things or people, other than Jesus, that are often worshiped today. Think prayerfully about this because these things or people may be so much a part of our lives that we don't even realize we are worshiping them.

_____

_____

_____

_____

With the exception of the first five years of my life, I have always struggled with my weight. When I was five years old, my tonsils were removed because they were constantly infected and swollen. Suddenly, I felt good and could eat comfortably. And did I eat! In the first year after my tonsillectomy, I gained 25 pounds. I went from a wisp of a child to pleasingly plump almost overnight. My mother was determined I would not be fat. In the late 1960s we had not entered the politically correct era, so she never used the word obese. I would not be FAT.

She watched my weight like a hawk watches its prey.

"You can't have that. It will make you FAT."

"That is FATTENING. You should not eat it."

"No, we don't eat bread because it is FATTENING."

"Potatoes and corn will make you FAT."

"Desserts are FATTENING."

I know she was only doing what she thought was best for me, but the message I internalized was "You are fat, and you don't need to eat that." Hear me! I was the one whose "understand-er" was broken. She said one thing, and I heard a totally different message. Over time, the message became louder and louder in my subconscious until one day I decided I would lose weight. When I was fifteen, I began dieting and lost fifteen pounds in the weeks between Thanksgiving and Christmas. The next summer I lost five more pounds and then five more and five more.

There was something of a high that came with losing weight and being thin. Before I even realized what was happening, I weighed less than 100 pounds. Yet I saw myself as F-A-T. My whole focus became losing more weight. In those days I allowed myself 600 calories each day. Six-hundred stinkin' calories. No one can live on six hundred calories, yet that seemed to be the magic amount of calories that would keep me alive and thin—barely alive and very thin.

My whole existence centered around counting calories, weighing myself, and looking in the mirror to make sure not a single ounce of fat had crept onto my slight frame. As you might imagine, after a few months of this, I was unable to function normally. I could not concentrate in college; I lost consciousness several times a day, and was a total mess. My body had become my god, and I had completely dethroned Jesus from my life. Thankfully, God sent a wise professor into my life to call me out on my illness and encourage me to seek help.

God sent the writer of Hebrews to these Christian Jews of antiquity to remind them not to place Moses on the throne of their hearts. Only Jesus should occupy the throne in the heart and life of a Christian. As we continue our look into chapter three of Hebrews, we find the writer taking a laser pointer and identifying the exact problem of these Christians.

Read Hebrews 3:7-19.

Look carefully at verses 8, 13 and 15. What word do you find used in each of these verses? (Hint: *skleryno*)

_____

_____

_____

_____

Now turn to Psalm 95 and read verses 7 through 11. Do you find anything familiar? If yes, what?

_____

_____

_____

_____

Consider this passage from *Word Biblical Commentary* about these corresponding verses from Psalm 95 and Hebrews 3:

> "The witness of Scripture is brought from the past into the present, contemporary with the experience of the readers. What was spoken or written concerning the desert generation centuries before has immediate relevance to the community addressed."[6]

These two passages refer to the Israelites turning away from God in the desert at Kadesh. They had refused to enter the Promised Land because of unbelief and hearts that were hardened toward God.

Glance at **Numbers 14.** Fill in the blanks**:**

- **Verse 11:** *The Lord said to Moses: How long will these people treat me with _____? How long will they refuse to _____ in me, in spite of all the miraculous signs I have performed among them?*

- ***Verse 23:*** *not one of them will ever see the land I promised on oath to their forefathers. No one who has treated me with _____ will ever see it.* [9]

What was this about? It was about hardened hearts and unbelief. God was charging the Israelites of Moses' day with rampant unbelief and contempt for Him. Our verses from Psalm 95 and Hebrews 3 are in direct response to the charges leveled by God on the Israelites. When they chose to believe men over God, they chose rebellion, disobedience, and contempt. The writer of Hebrews is imploring his readers not to make the same choice the Israelites of Moses' day made. "Believe in Jesus Christ and worship Him only," he urges them. "Yes, Moses was faithful, but you have your eyes on the wrong person. Don't harden your hearts and place Moses above Jesus."

In the days when I battled anorexia, I had taken my eyes off Jesus and put them on myself. Every time I take my eyes off Jesus and put them on any thing or person other than Jesus, my heart will immediately begin to become hardened. Oh, I may not realize that is what is happening, but it is. For example, when I find justification for skipping my quiet time with the Lord, my prayer life becomes weak and ineffective. In short, my relationship with Jesus is hindered because of the hardening of my heart—the unbelief in my heart.

What about you? Have you ever been in this place of a hardened heart like the Israelites of antiquity? Most of us have, and if we would admit it—it is an uncomfortable place to be. Why? Because the Holy Spirit will constantly be calling and wooing you back. He will not be still if one of His children has strayed.

If you are in this place of unbelief and hardness of heart, I encourage you to give it up. The consequences of a hardened heart are unpleasant, and sometimes downright miserable! God will rebuke you until you come back to Him if you are His child. Don't make it hard on yourself. Admit your hardness of heart to God and ask Him to forgive you and draw you back—close to Him. Use today's Meditation Moment to do this.

MEDITATION MOMENT:

Please do not skip over this time. I am asking you to enter into a few moments of prayer and listening for God's voice. Perhaps you are not aware of any unbelief in your heart, but you want to make certain there is not a hardened part of your heart hidden even to you. This is the moment for you to ask God to reveal anything that is displeasing to Him. Perhaps you know you have hardened your heart toward Jesus, and you desire to move past this place. This is your moment too. I am going to lead you in a time of guided prayer. You can certainly make this prayer your own or use what I am offering. What is important is that you do

whatever it takes to confess the unbelief in your heart and re-ignite your relationship with Jesus. Will you join me?

First, express to the Lord exactly where you are right now…at this moment. If you feel far away from Him, tell Him. If you feel fearful, tell Him. If you are not sure if there is unbelief in your heart but you want to find out, ask Him to show you. Whatever you are feeling in this moment, tell Him about it. He already knows; He simply wants you to be honest with Him.

Second, ask Jesus to forgive you for hardening your heart toward Him. It is so easy! Just tell Him you are sorry, and mean it with all your heart.

Third, because you do not want to go back to that place of unbelief again, ask Him to help you fill your heart with love for Him and a desire to stay faithful to Him.

Finally, in the space below journal about what just happened. Place today's date at the end of your entry. End by taking time to thank the Lord for His faithfulness to you.

Day 4 – Give It a Rest!

Today I want us to do something new and different—a word study. I have never used it as a teaching tool in writing a Bible study; however, I sense the Holy Spirit calling us to focus on one particular word in the first eleven verses of Hebrews 4. The word we will examine today is "*rest.*" In our English language this word re*st* has numerous meanings, and the same is true in the Greek. In fact, in the Greek there are several words that mean *rest,* and today we will explore each of them. First, though, let's think about what *rest* means to us.

What comes to mind when you hear the word rest? Don't think too hard on this one…just write down whatever comes to mind.

_____

_____

_____

_____

Webster's Collegiate Dictionary defines rest as: "a bodily state characterized by minimal functional and metabolic activities; a freedom from activity or labor; a state of motionlessness or inactivity." [7]

Let's see what spiritual gems about rest we can mine from our word study in Hebrews 4.

Read **Hebrews 4:1-11 (NIV1984)** below and circle or highlight each usage of the word *rest*.

> *1 Therefore, since the promise of entering his rest still stands, let us be careful that none of you be found to have fallen short of it. 2 For we also have had the gospel preached to us, just as they did; but the message they heard was of no value to them, because those who heard did not combine it with faith. 3 Now we who have believed enter that rest, just as God has said, "So I declared on oath in my anger, 'They shall never enter my rest.'" And yet his work has been finished since the creation of the world. 4 For somewhere he has spoken about the seventh day in these words: "And on the seventh day God rested from all his work." 5 And again in the passage above he says, "They shall never enter my rest." 6 It still remains that some will enter that rest, and those who formerly had the gospel preached to them did not go in, because of their disobedience. 7 Therefore God again set a certain day, calling it Today, when a long time*

later he spoke through David, as was said before: "Today, if you hear his voice, do not harden your hearts." 8 For if Joshua had given them rest, God would not have spoken later about another day. 9 There remains, then, a Sabbath-rest for the people of God; 10 for anyone who enters God's rest also rests from his own work, just as God did from his. 11 Let us, therefore, make every effort to enter that rest, so that no one will fall by following their example of disobedience.

In these eleven verses we find the word *rest* used eleven times. When God repeats a word that often in such a short space, He wants us to take notice of it. In these eleven verses three different Greek words are used for rest.

The first word used for *rest* is *katapausis,* and it is, by far, the most frequently used—seven times in eleven verses. Let's consider the meaning of it: "To make to cease. The act or state of resting, ceasing from labor." [8] *The Lifeway Online Study Bible* adds more to the definition. "Also, a putting to rest, calming of the winds, a resting place. Metaphorically, the heavenly blessedness in which God dwells, and of which he has promised to make persevering believers in Christ partakers after the toils and trials of life on earth are ended." [9]

The next most frequently used word is *katapauo,* and it is used three times in this passage. It has the same meaning as the previous word, but it also hints at giving rest. Words that are related to this word mean to rest inwardly, to relax from toil, to be quiet, still. *The Lifeway Online Study Bible* offers these additional meanings: "to lead to a quiet abode, to still, restrain, to cause (one striving to do something) to desist." [10]

The final word used for rest in Hebrews 4 is *sabbatismos,* and it means "a keeping Sabbath, the blessed rest from toils and troubles looked for in the age to come by the true worshippers of God and true Christians." [11]

I would like to use the remainder of this day to focus on one particular portion of the definition of the word *katapausis,* and that is "ceasing from labor." Please understand that I am not advocating quitting your job. If you are like me, you have grown rather accustomed to eating and living indoors, and to continue in that lifestyle we must work. I want us to think about the issue of rest from the standpoint of our salvation. I believe we are safe in exploring this path because ancient, as well as modern, Judaism is based on the works of a person. Recall that the author of Hebrews was seeking to remind his Jewish Christian house church of the dangers of returning to the works of Judaism when they already had received Christ and the work He did on the cross. **Hebrews 4:10** is key in understanding what the author was trying to convey. Consider this verse from the *New Living Translation*: *For all who have entered into God's rest have rested from their labors, just as God did after creating the world.*

Perhaps you have participated in one of the "read the Bible through in a year" programs at some point in your life. You begin with great momentum in Genesis and learn all about the patriarchs: Noah, Abraham, Isaac, Jacob, and Moses. Then you run into the brick wall called Leviticus. Law-after-law-after-law. A law here, a law there, everywhere a law, law. Oh mercy! It is hard enough to read them, but just imagine the Hebrews of antiquity trying to *keep* all those laws!

Let's get just a tiny taste of what the ancient Hebrews had to endure as we take a quick glance at some portions of Leviticus. Please don't skip over this part because it sets the stage for the rest of the day of study. God promises that His Word never returns void—and that includes Leviticus.

In **Leviticus 1:1-2** what did God require to be brought as an offering to Him?

_____

_____

_____

Leviticus 4:27-29 gives the requirements for the atonement for unintentional sin. What was the sinner required to do in verse 29 in order to find atonement for his sin?

_____

_____

_____

Did you get that? The person bringing the offering had to slay the goat himself! Eww!!

The Jewish people could only eat certain kinds of animals. What guidelines are given with regard to these animals in **Leviticus 11:2-3**?

_____

_____

_____

Leviticus 12 provides laws regarding the purification of a woman after she gives birth to a child. What restrictions were the women placed under after giving birth according to verses **1-5**?

_____

_____

_____

According to **Leviticus 13:42-46**, a man with a reddish-white sore on his bald-head or forehead was considered to have an infectious disease. What was the man required to do in verses 45-46?

_____

_____

_____

Leviticus 19:19 details three "do nots". What are they?

_____

_____

_____

Can you imagine having to keep up with all these laws and requirements in order to find acceptance with God? It was impossible, yet the Jewish people tried. They still try today—prayers, offerings, works, good deeds, more offerings, more prayers, more works, more good deeds. It is endless striving for acceptance and salvation that will never come through works. The Greek word for "work or works" is *ergon* and it means "business; employment; that in which any one is occupied; undertaking; ***an act, deed, thing done***."[12] The bottom line is that no one can work his or her way into salvation. The sole purpose of God giving the Law was to prove to the Jewish people that they would not find complete and permanent atonement through keeping the Law. There had to be a *BETTER* way.

Let's consider what the apostle Paul had to say about the law or the Old Covenant and also about a better way to God. Fill in the blanks below.

- **Romans 3:19-20 (NKJV):** *Now we know that whatever the law says, it says to those who are under the law, so that every mouth may be silenced and the whole world held accountable to _____. Therefore no one will be declared _____ in his sight by observing the _____; rather, through the law we become conscious of _____.*

- **Romans 8:3-4 (NIV1984):** *For what the law was _____ to do in that it was weakened by the sinful nature, God did by sending His own _____ in the likeness of sinful man to be a sin _____. And so He condemned sin in sinful man, in order that the righteous _____ of the law might be fully met in us, who do not live according to the sinful nature but according to the Spirit.*

- **Galatians 2:16 (NIV1984):** *Know that a man is not justified by _____ _____ _____, but by _____ in Jesus Christ. So we, too, have put our faith in Christ Jesus that we may be justified by faith in Christ and not by observing the law, because by observing the law _____ will be justified (NIV1984).*

It is only through faith in Jesus Christ that we gain salvation. No works, no labor, no striving, no laws to keep—just a simple prayer from the depths of a repentant heart.

Jesus, thank You for dying on the cross to pay the debt I owed for my sin. Forgive me for my rebellion and disobedience to You, Lord. Come live in my heart and one day take me to live with You. Amen.

It really is that simple. Why do we try to make it hard?

MEDITATION MOMENT:

Turn to **Isaiah 30:15** and write it in the space provided. It is a beautiful reminder of what God requires of us. The Hebrew word translated "trust" in this verse means "there is nothing more one can do." Let's not be like the ancient Israelites and "have none of it." Let's fully live in the assurance of our salvation and forsake all the striving we tend to do in order to be accepted by God.

Day 5 – Not Just Another Book on the Shelf

I warned you from the beginning that we would move quickly through certain parts of Hebrews and we have done so in our first four days of study. Today, however, we will apply the brakes and camp out on two verses at the end of chapter four. First, though, I want to put these verses in perspective with what we have studied thus far. As has been my practice in the past, somewhere in week one I always include the pathway to salvation through faith in Jesus Christ. We examined that on Day 2. It is only when we are in a relationship with Jesus Christ, who died to provide payment for our sin, that we fully understand He is the *better* thing in the book of Hebrews. I hope you have asked Jesus to be your best friend. Once you make a commitment to Jesus, you are saved. You have Jesus living in your heart and His Spirit living within you to help you make wise decisions throughout your life.

That is only the beginning, however. In order to grow in your relationship with Him and take full advantage of all He offers you here on this earth, there is more for you to consider—just as in a marriage, the wedding is not the end—it is only the beginning. The bride and groom promise to love each other and are married, but they must share and learn to trust each other more each day for their relationship to deepen—so it is with Jesus.

How do you grow in your relationship with Christ? By talking with Him and listening to Him, through prayer and reading His love letter to you. His love letter to you is the Bible, and He has much to say to us. Today I want us to search the Scriptures to find out why the Bible should be important to us. We will also hear the testimony of one of my friends who has been changed by the Word of God. My goal is for all of this to encourage a hunger and thirst for God's Word in your heart.

Turn to **Psalm 119:9 (NIV1984)** and fill in the blanks: *How can a young man _____ his way pure? By_____ according to your_____.*

Now, put this verse in your own words. What does the verse say to you personally?

_____

_____

_____

_____

What this verse says to me is that the Bible, the Word of God, has the power to transform people if they will read, understand, and apply its principles. I know this is true. It happened to me. You may be thinking something like this: "Why all this talk about an ancient, boring book, Leah? You talk about it like it was a person and able to impact people's lives."

Good question. I used to think that very thing about the Bible…until I started studying it. I hope to prove to you that the Bible is alive and able to change your life just like it changed mine. Sounds good, huh? So how can a book, an ancient book, change a person? Let's look at our focal verses to discover the answer to this question.

Read **Hebrews 4:12-13** and answer the following questions.

Let's go back a bit to our high school English days. What two adjectives are used to describe the word of God in the first sentence of verse 12?

_____

_____

_____

_____

What instrument of warfare is the Word of God compared to in the second sentence of verse 12?

_____

_____

_____

What are the things the Word of God divides in verse 12?

_____

_____

_____

_____

What are the things the Word of God judges in verse 12?

_____

_____

_____

At first glance, verse 13 does not seem to fit very well with verse 12. In light of verse 12, what do you believe the significance of verse 13 is?

_____

_____

_____

The Greek word used in verse 12 for active is *energes*. It comes from two words: *en* meaning "in" and *ergon* meaning "work." Consider the meaning of this word: "*Energes* was used in extra-biblical Greek to describe freshly plowed land ready for cultivation, a mill in working condition, and drugs effective in bringing a cure. The word of God contains a potency which when unleashed successfully accomplishes what gets results and can actualize or realize things." [13]

I think we can all understand the part pertaining to medications. When you are sick and go to the doctor, he or she will write a prescription to help cure your illness. You take the prescription to the pharmacy where the pharmacist fills it, you pay for it, and take it home. Up to this point, the medication in the bottle is just a substance designed to cure a specific problem. The medication has the power to cure your illness, but you must choose to activate that power. Until you actually take the medication from the bottle, put it into your mouth, and swallow, it is has no power. The power is unleashed in your body to cure your illness when the medication is taken.

So it is with the Bible. As long as it lies unread on your shelf or nightstand, it has no power to change your life; however, when it is opened and read, power is unleashed that will produce a heart change in your life.

Turn to **Isaiah 55:10-11.** Answer the following questions from this passage:

To what is the word of God compared?

_____

_____

_____

What are we told is the purpose of the rain and snow?

_____

_____

_____

What three things does God promise about His Word?

_____

_____

_____

_____

God's Word, the Bible, is powerful. Psalm 119 is about the Word of God and how it can change hearts and lives. Let's take a look at the advantages available to a person who reads God's Word and believes it. In the following verses, several different words are used to identify God's Word, the Bible. Words such as laws, statues, commands, and precepts all refer to the Bible.

Read each verse from Psalm 119 listed below. Note what advantage or benefit is gained from believing God's Word.

Verse 11 –

_____

_____

_____

Verse 28 –

_____

_____

_____

Verse 52 –

_____

_____

_____

Verse 66 –

_____

_____

_____

Verse 98 –

_____

_____

_____

Verse 105 –

_____

_____

_____

Verse 154 –

_____

_____

_____

I especially love Psalm 119:98. I want to be wiser…yes, wiser than my enemy. So, how does this work in real life? Because really, if it is only theory on the page, what good is it to you and me? In order to illustrate the power of God's Word, I am excited to share my friend Lydia's story with you.

I met Lydia one day at church. I had stopped by to prepare the room where I would lead my first study, _From the Trash Pile to the Treasure Chest: Creating a Godly Legacy_. As I chatted with my pastor, he said, "I have someone I think you should meet." He went on to tell me a bit of Lydia's story.

Lydia, a paralegal who lived in Florida, had grown up in a religion considered by many to be a cult. One of Lydia's clients was a man named Scott. Scott, a devout Christian, sensed Lydia was not a true believer in Jesus Christ. Over the months Lydia worked on Scott's legal case, Scott gently, yet without apology, witnessed to Lydia. By Lydia's own admission, it took "a while" for her to fall under conviction from the Holy Spirit. One day Scott told Lydia he had some Bible verses he wanted her to read. Scott pointed Lydia to Hebrews 1.

Lydia says, "He had me read Hebrews the first chapter. I knew as soon as I read it, that my former life had been lies. I realized that Jesus couldn't be an angel like I had always been taught. The verses in Hebrews 1 tell us that Jesus is higher than the angels. In the same chapter it also tells us the angels worship Jesus. It was like the switch had been flipped, and I saw light at that point. I realized I didn't have the right view of who Jesus was. I knew I couldn't continue living in the darkness. That was the day I received God's salvation. It was really the most amazing moment of my life. I began to cry and sob—yet I felt so calm. I know it sounds strange, but it was the most life-changing event I've ever experienced."

Because of the first chapter of Hebrews, Lydia came to know Jesus as her Lord and Savior. She also gained a second benefit. Lydia and Scott, both single, fell in love with each other. I attended their wedding in 2011, and it was a precious time of celebration.

Lydia's newfound faith did not come without a steep price, however. Because Lydia accepted Jesus as her Lord and left the religion of her family, she has been completely disowned by her parents and extended family. No one from her family attended her wedding.

Lydia explains, "My family disowned me in hopes of teaching me what I've lost. And believe me, I still grieve for them. I know their hope was that I'd come running home and leave my relationship with God. Both Scott and I write them and try to minister to them. It is hard. It is very difficult emotionally to know they won't respond, but one of my favorite scriptures is Hebrews 6:10: "God is not unrighteous, so as to forget the love we show for Him." I remind myself of this verse when I get sad or start missing my family. I receive blessings everyday. Just this week I received a little card from my dad. So, although the shunning hasn't lifted, I see God working in him. I am blessed." [14]

Friend, I want to encourage you to dive deeply into the Word of God and learn what God has to teach you. It will change your life just as it changed Lydia's. You may regret many things in your life, but studying God's Word and drawing closer to Jesus will never be one of them. The Word of God truly is alive and active. I challenge you to feast on it for yourself.

MEDITATION MOMENT:

Journal about a time or circumstance when the Word of God made an impact on your life and heart. If you cannot think of a situation, spend some time asking the Lord to use the Bible in your life in the coming days in such a way that you know, without a doubt, you have heard from God.

May I Serve You?

For our dessert this week, I turn to my friend, Janice, whose recipe for Apple Dumpling Cobbler has become a Bible study favorite at my house. It is full of fruit, nuts, butter, and crescent rolls….the four main food groups, right? If you like apple cobbler or apple dumplings, you will be in heaven with this recipe. Just like last week's recipe, this one is super easy and quick to make, yet it will have your guests begging for a second helping. I recommend a steaming cup of Caramel Apple Cider with a generous helping of whipped cream and extra caramel on top.

RECIPE

Apple Dumpling Cobbler

8 oz. can crescent rolls

2 large Granny Smith apples, peeled and quartered

2/3 cup orange juice

2/3 cup sugar

2/3 cup butter

2 teaspoons sugar

1 teaspoon cinnamon

2/3 cup pecan pieces

Unroll crescent rolls and separate. Wrap each quarter of apple in a crescent roll. Place in a lightly greased 9x13 baking dish. Bring orange juice, butter, and 2/3 cup of sugar to boil in a saucepan; then pour over apple dumplings. Stir together 2 teaspoons sugar and 1 teaspoon cinnamon and sprinkle on dumplings. Scatter pecans on top. Bake 25 minutes at 350 degrees. Can be served a la mode.

WEEK 2 — A Better Priest — The Reserve Blend

The Catholic Church became an orphan of sorts when Pope Benedict XVI resigned. It was shocking to the Catholic Church, because it is the first time in six hundred years that a pope has not served until his death. Benedict cited his age and declining health as the reason he was choosing to step down. Although I have not had a chance to chat with my Catholic friends concerning their feelings about Benedict's retirement, the fact that he *willingly* stepped away from a position of power and worldwide influence, in favor of a life of prayer and solitude, speaks of his humility and devotion to the Lord. He appears to have a God focus.

There was another who stepped aside from an even greater position of priestly power and influence. His name was Jesus. This week, we journey back into the Old Testament to visit with the Levite priest who served in the wilderness tabernacle. His was not a glamorous job, nor was it particularly easy; however, it was a job that he and his brethren were called to by God. He served as an intermediary between the Jewish people and Jehovah God. The work of the Old Testament priest foreshadowed the work that Jesus would do on the cross almost two millennia later. Our study this week will bring to light evidence that Jesus, the Son of God, is truly the better priest.

Day 1 — A Glance Back at the Old

For many of us with southern blood running through our veins, the only choice in soft drinks is Coca Cola® products. Coca Cola® money built many buildings and landmarks in Atlanta, and the presence of the company looms large in the area. The company is zealous and dogmatic about its products.

In the mid 1990's I rode with a co-worker from Emory University to a meeting at Coca Cola® headquarters in downtown Atlanta. When we pulled up to the main gate at the entrance to the property, a guard approached our car. The first words out of his mouth were not, "What is your name?" or "Who are you here to see?" No. The first words out of his mouth were, "You cannot bring *that* onto the property." My friend said, "Bring what?" The man pointed to the Mountain Dew® can in her console and said, "*That*. You cannot bring a Pepsi® product onto the property." Without argument, she relinquished her partially consumed can of Mountain Dew® to the guard for disposal. Coca Cola® is serious about their business.

In the 1980's, Coca Cola® Inc made a costly mistake when they decided it was time for an update to their flagship product. The emergence of "New Coke" to the market brought forth a near primal scream from generations of ardent, die-hard Coke fans. "New Coke" was a disaster. It did not take long for the Coca Cola® corporate office to announce the withdrawal of "New Coke" from the American market. Over the years, original Coke® has been the mainstay of the company, proving that not everything labeled "new" is a better thing.

Today, however, we study something labeled "new" that truly is better. As we continue our study of the book of Hebrews, we find the author reminding his readers of the Old Testament priesthood and the improvements that Jesus, our High Priest, brought to the priestly office.

For context, let's take a look back at the Old Testament priesthood and be reminded of the reasons God established it. Today, you will be reading from several places in the Old Testament. Look up each reference from the Old Testament and answer the question based on it. Each question will build on the previous one, so you can understand the origins and job descriptions of the Old Testament priesthood. Let's get started.

Exodus 28:1: According to God's instructions, who did Moses appoint as priests for the wilderness tabernacle? Please write out the names. I want you to be familiar with them.

_____

_____

_____

Numbers 16:40: Only descendants of what man were to be appointed as priests among the Israelites?

_____

_____

_____

Leviticus 9:7: Aaron, as High Priest, was instructed by Moses to offer sin sacrifices for whose atonement?

_____

_____

_____

Leviticus 4:1-2: Fill in the blank: _____ a*nyone sins uninten-tionally and does what is forbidden in any of the Lord's command*s—The entire fourth chapter of Leviticus details the required sin offerings for unintentional sin in the Israelite community. Verse 3 tells us that this sin offering was also applicable to the priests. Knowing this offering was for unintentional sin, do you think it would have been a one-time offering? Why or why not?

_____

_____

_____

Exodus: 29:38: In addition to the sin offerings for themselves and the people of Israel, the priests were required to offer a variety of other offerings and sacrifices to satisfy the requirements of God's law. How often does this verse tell us sacrifice offerings were made?

_____

_____

_____

The furnishings for the Old Testament tabernacle are detailed in the diagram below, as well as in the latter half of the book of Exodus. Do you see anything to sit on within the Old Testament tabernacle? [15]

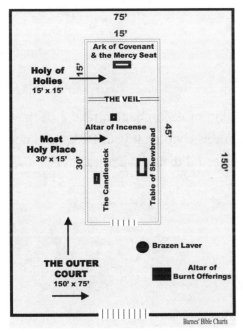

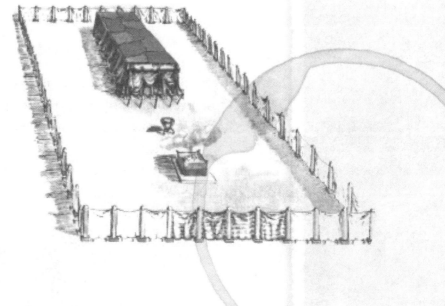

Please write out **Hebrews 10:11**.

_____

_____

_____

Read **Hebrews 10:10-14** for context. To whom does "this priest" refer in verse 12? What position does this priest assume that is different than the priest in verse 11?

_____

_____

_____

The fact that the Old Testament priest never sat in the tabernacle tells us that his work was never finished. He had to keep coming back, offering the same sacrifices over and over for the sin of the people. Contrast that with the BETTER priest who sat down at the right hand of God once His work was finished. That's huge, people. HUGE!! A finished work. Finished. Completed. Never to be done again. One time for all. Now, that is worth shouting about!

Numbers 20:28: Whose highly significant death took place in this verse?

_____

_____

_____

If your Bible has headings at the beginning of each chapter, take a peek at **Leviticus 10** and note what happened in this chapter. If your Bible does not have chapter or section headings, read verses 1-2 to find the story.

_____

_____

_____

Okay, let's recap what we learned in these verses because it will be important information as we move forward this week, learning about the BETTER priesthood of Jesus.

The Old Testament priesthood was a job, appointed by God, from which the priests ultimately retired—either because they reached the age of retirement or they died. Everything about this priesthood was limited. Because the priests were mortal men, they were required to offer sacrifices for their own sin. Although the priesthood served a purpose in God's economy, it fell far short of accomplishing everything God intended. Did God make a mistake when He ordained the Old Testament priesthood? Not at all! He accomplished exactly what He desired to accomplish, which was to show the Israelites their need of a BETTER priest. Tomorrow we will catch a glimpse of that BETTER priest as we visit with Abraham.

MEDITATION MOMENT:

All too often we, as Christians, settle for less than God's best for our lives. Begin to consider and ask God to show you if there is an area of your life where you stand in need of God's better solution. Perhaps it is in your thought life, your job, your earthly relationships, your finances, or your physical health. Spend some time journaling about what God shows you in this regard.

Day 2 – May I Introduce You to Melchizedek?

Have you ever met someone who just seemed to have it all together and have everything going for her? She was beautiful, popular, financially successful, had a nice home, lived a godly life, had a husband who adored her and children who were obedient and well behaved. Basically, she was too good to be true!

Meet Melchizedek! He appears to be that "too good to be true" person in Scripture. Today we will visit with Melchizedek in both the Old and New Testaments. Let's consider Melchizedek in his first appearance in Scripture. Turn to **Genesis 14 and read verses 18-20**.

Note everything you learn about Melchizedek from these verses.

_____

_____

_____

Now, turn to **Hebrews chapter 7 and read verses 1-10**.

Note anything NEW you learned about Melchizedek from these verses.

_____

_____

_____

One of the first highly significant facts you should have noted is that Melchizedek was King of Salem, but he was also a priest of God Most High. In ancient times, this combination was unheard of—no king performed the duties of a priest. Recall from yesterday that the priestly line was from Aaron, the brother of Moses. Both Aaron and Moses were descendants of Levi. Hence, the Old Testament priesthood was often called the Levitical priesthood.

What does **Hebrews 7:3** tell us about the lineage of Melchizedek?

_____

_____

_____

Interesting, huh? First allow me to tell you that scholars disagree on who Melchizedek was. Some believe he was a Canaanite priest-king, while others see him as a pre-incarnate appearance of Jesus Christ. Consider two quotes from *Word Biblical Commentary* about Melchizedek's lineage:

A "radical difference existed between the priesthood of Melchizedek and the more familiar Levitical line of priests." [16]

Oh yes, there was truly a radical difference in the two priesthoods. Again, *Word Biblical Commentary* speaks to the importance of this.

> "The silence of scripture concerning Melchizedek's parents and family line is stressed by the writer [of Hebrews] to amplify the concept of the uniqueness of his priesthood, and not as a proof of that uniqueness. It implies that Melchizedek's priesthood was not established upon the external circumstances of birth and descent. It was based on the call of God and not on the hereditary process by which the Levitical priesthood was sustained. Without a recorded priestly genealogy, Melchizedek could not have qualified for the Levitical priesthood. Nevertheless, this man was priest of God Most High, and Abraham recognized his dignity." [17]

I could give you my opinion at this point about who Melchizedek was, but Word Biblical Commentary does a much better job, so please humor me for one more quote concerning Melchizedek.

> "Melchizedek's sudden appearance and equally sudden disappearance from recorded history evoked the notion of eternity, which was only prefigured in Melchizedek but was realized in Christ. Consequently, Melchizedek foreshadows the priesthood of Christ at that point where it is most fundamentally different from the Levitical priesthood." [18]

Have you ever had one of those "Twilight Zone" moments where you think "I've been here before" or "I know I've met that person before," but you are certain you never have? That must have been exactly what Jesus thought when He came to earth and lived as a man; however, He had been here before and He knew he had. He was the creator of it all and was intimately familiar with His creation. His purpose was to foreshadow to the patriarchs a BETTER priesthood.

At this point you should be asking yourself why a BETTER priesthood was needed. That is the question we will consider tomorrow.

MEDITATION MOMENT:

Today let's do a less intense Meditation Moment. We have studied about Melchizedek and considered the idea that He might have been a pre-incarnate appearing of Jesus. That is one of those "I'll ask Jesus about that when I get to heaven" issues. I think we all have things about which we are curious, but we will not know the answer until we step into heaven. List one or two things that you are eager to find the answer to when you arrive in heaven.

_____

_____

_____

_____

_____

_____

_____

_____

Day 3 – Why Do We Need a Better Priest?

One of the iconic images of the 1960s presidency of John F. Kennedy was of the President sitting in the Oval office, working at his desk. The Resolute desk is an ornate piece of furniture with a door that opens in the front. When one views the picture, almost immediately the eye is drawn to the bottom of the photograph where the President's young son, John-John, has opened the small door beneath the desk and is peeking out at reporters and photographers. The picture is one that bespeaks familiarity and unhindered access.

Only the Kennedy family had privileged and unhindered access to President Kennedy. Needless to say, if anyone else had tried to crawl beneath the President's desk, the Secret Service would have been on him like white on rice. This is the privilege that goes with being "family."

At one time, man had free and unhindered access to God, but that was destroyed by disobedience. As we consider the issue of the need for a better priest than that available to the Israelites, we must go back to the beginning and understand how the need came about. In Genesis 3:8 we are told that God was walking in the Garden of Eden in the cool of the day. It seems reasonable to think this might have been a habit of God's—God and His prized creation taking a walk and catching up on the day. The only problem was that on this particular day, man was nowhere to be found. Man was not lost, but rather, he and Eve were hiding.

Why in the world would they hide? For the very same reason you and I try to hide from God on occasion—they had been disobedient. They had done the one thing God had expressly forbidden them to do. They had eaten from the tree of the knowledge of good and evil, and their eyes had been opened. Now, their disobedience to God's command would result in consequences far worse than they could ever have imagined.

What does **Genesis 3:23-24** tell us were the consequences of Adam and Eve's disobedience?

_____

_____

_____

_____

Adam and Eve lost free access to the presence of God in the Garden of Eden. They were banished from the garden and forced to work the land in order to provide for themselves. Now, God's presence in the garden would be guarded by cherubim and a flaming sword. No human would enter the Garden ever again.

Fast forward several hundred years and we find Abraham being called by God to go to a land that would ultimately belong to his descendants. Out of this call, the Jewish nation is birthed. A few hundred more years and Moses is called by God to lead the Jewish people out of slavery in Egypt and into the Promised Land. Since Adam and Eve were cast out of the Garden of Eden, man had not had free access to God's presence. God would speak to certain individuals, but this was pretty rare.

As Moses and the Israelites begin the journey out of Egypt, God instructs Moses to build a tabernacle in the desert where His presence would dwell. Here we see God's attempt to re-establish relationship with man.

Fill in the blanks from **Exodus 25:8 (NIV1984)**—*Then have them make a _____ for me, and I will _____ among them.*

God was reaching out to humans, yet we see that only a select few men ever got to be in the presence of God in this tabernacle—this happened on the Day of Atonement. In Leviticus 16 the Bible gives us details about the Day of Atonement. Answer the following questions regarding this special day of the Jews.

Read **Leviticus 16:2**. Could Aaron, the high priest, enter the Holy of Holies where the presence of the Lord dwelled among the Israelites any time he wanted?

_____

_____

_____

What would be the consequences of entering the Holy of Holies without the approval of God?

_____

_____

_____

Was anyone else authorized to enter the Holy of Holies according to verse 2?

_____

According to **Leviticus 16:34**, how often was Aaron authorized by God to enter His presence in the Holy of Holies?

_____

What was the purpose of Aaron's visit to the Holy of Holies?

_____

_____

Aaron, or whoever was serving as high priest, was the only man allowed into the Holy of Holies and then only one time each year. In a sense, the people's access to God was somewhat re-established, but it was severely limited. The ordinary Joe or Jane still had no access to God.

Perhaps you are wondering why I am making such a big deal out of people's access to God. We all need to understand that God is a God of relationship. He does not need our company, but He desires it. He wants to speak to us and have us talk to Him. He longs to give us good gifts, as well as the ultimate gift of His presence; however, once sin entered into people's lives, they were separated from God by it. You see, God is perfect and perfectly holy. In Him is no sin and because of that He cannot be in relationship with sin. So, the moment humans sinned in the garden, God knew He would have to find a way to restore that relationship.

This is where our need for a new High Priest—a BETTER priest—comes into the picture. Turn to **Hebrews 7:11-28** and let's see what insight this passage provides.

Do you recall from Day 1 of this week of study that the priest in the earthly tabernacle had to continually offer daily sacrifices for his own sin and the sin of the people? Since God required continual sacrifice, we can reasonably assume that those sacrifices did not completely cover the sin of the person offering the sacrifice. His sin was covered only until he sinned again. If I had been the one offering the sacrifice for my sin, I pretty much would have had to move into the tabernacle because I would need to offer a sacrifice pretty frequently—maybe you can relate.

Hebrews 7:11 addresses this need specifically. The first two words of the verse are particularly important. "If perfection…." What does that mean? The Greek

word for perfection is *teleiosis,* and it means "the state or attainment of perfection; to complete, fulfillment." [19] The writer of Hebrews is asking that if were possible to have complete salvation through the Old Testament priesthood where sacrifices were offered continually, why would it have been necessary for God to send a BETTER High Priest in the person of Jesus? Bottom line: the Levitical priesthood was flawed from the start. Not because God made a mistake, because God does not make mistakes. Rather, it was flawed in order to point out the need for a BETTER priest—One who could provide perfection or complete salvation.

The Old Testament priests were human with all the human limitations we might imagine. They sinned, they died, they grew old, they could only offer temporary sacrifices. The BETTER High Priest would be limited in none of these ways.

Fill in the blanks from **Hebrews 7:26-28** (NIV1984):

Such a _____ _____ meets

our need—one who is _____, blameless, pure, set apart

from _____, exalted above the heavens. Unlike

the other high priests, he does not need to offer sacrifices day after day, first for his

_____ _____, and then for the sins

of the people. He sacrificed for their sins _____ when

he offered himself. For the law appoints as high priests men who are weak; but the

oath, which came after the law, appointed the _____,

who has been made _____ forever.

Remember the word "perfection" back in Hebrews 7:11? That Greek word *teleiosis* is derived from the Greek word for *perfect* that was used at the end of Hebrews 7:28 just now. The writer of Hebrews is telling us that God sent Jesus, the BETTER High Priest, because He brought perfection, completion, and fulfillment. No other sacrifice would be needed because this High Priest came to offer the ultimate Sacrifice—Himself. Never again would an innocent lamb or goat need to be slaughtered to cover the sin of all mankind. Jesus would be the final, perfect sacrifice to cover the sin of all people. Tomorrow we will learn more about our BETTER priest.

MEDITATION MOMENT:

Think about your closest and most intimate earthly relationship. Perhaps it is with your spouse, your best friend, or a parent. Do you remember a time when the relationship was strained or hindered by disobedience and sin? How did you feel? Did that person refuse to talk to you or have anything to do with you? Were angry words exchanged? When sin comes between God and us, there is a hindrance to the relationship because God cannot fellowship with sin and disobedience. Yet, He desires a restoration of the relationship with us. This is why He sent the BETTER priest, Jesus, to offer the ultimate sacrifice that would restore our relationship with God. Take a moment and ask the Holy Spirit to show you any hindrance to your relationship with God. Now, ask Him to help you confess it to the Lord and get rid of it.

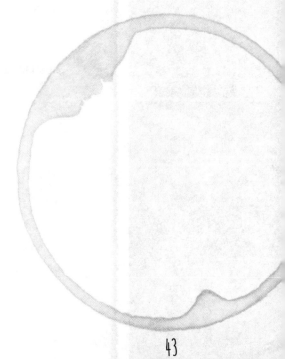

Day 4 – Jesus, the Better High Priest

The word *better* suggests the need for improvement in something or someone. Consider the meaning of the word from the *Encarta Dictionary*: "indicating that somebody, something, or an action is superior in some way to something or somebody else or is an improvement upon a situation; more acceptable; of greater quality; improved in health; to higher standard; preferably; surpass something; improve self or thing; superior person." [20]

What thoughts or feelings does the word *better* bring up for you? There is no right or wrong answer for this. Just put down the first things that come to your mind.

_____

_____

_____

To the religious elite of the first century, the idea of a better high priest was nothing short of heresy. How dare anyone suggest a deficiency in the priesthood! Yet that is exactly what the author of the book of Hebrews does. The Jewish Christians of that day would have been familiar with the strengths and weaknesses of the priesthood. This week in our study, we have examined the Old Testament priesthood as well as a different kind of priest embodied in Melchizedek. Day 3 allowed us to consider why a better priesthood was needed. Today, we are going to see how Jesus, the BETTER priest, perfectly fit the bill.

Please turn to Hebrews 4, where we will begin our study for the day. Read **Hebrews 4:14—5:10**.

From this passage please list every qualification you can find that would make Jesus the BETTER High Priest.

_____

_____

_____

_____

Let's study a few of these in closer detail with the goal of strengthening our faith in Jesus' ability to be our priest before God. This was the exact goal of the writer of Hebrews: to show the early Jewish Christians that Jesus was the better priest and He could provide a more perfect path to God,—*a great high priest who has gone through the heavens, Jesus the Son of God.* (**Hebrews 4:14,** NIV1984**).

In this verse we see two very significant pieces of information pointing to Jesus as the BETTER priest. First, Jesus was a High Priest who had passed through the heavens. In order to understand the significance of this, we must look once again to a drawing of the Old Testament tabernacle. [21]

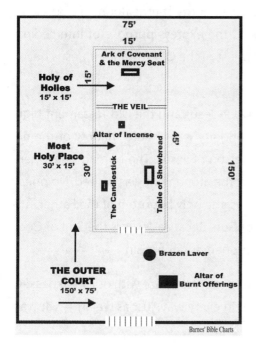

Answer the following questions (True or False) based on the picture above:

T F   The outer court of the temple, which held the bronze altar and the bronze laver, was an area the high priest must pass through in order to enter the tabernacle.

T F   The high priest was able to bypass the Holy Place (which held the table of showbread, lampstand and altar of incense) on his way into the Holy of Holies.

T F   The Holy of Holies, where the presence of God dwelt in the Old Testament tabernacle, was a place accessible to anyone who wanted to go in.

The Old Testament high priest had to pass through the outer court and the Holy Place in order to enter into the Holy of Holies where the presence of God dwelt. It was only after he had passed through the place of sacrifice and cleansing (outer court) as well as the place of provision and offering (Holy Place) that he could offer the yearly sacrifice for the sin of the people of Israel. Once he offered the sacrifice, the high priest had to leave the Holy of Holies. He could not return for another year, until the Day of Atonement. Year after year, the Day of Atonement came and went— every year until Jesus died.

Jesus, the BETTER High Priest, had to pass through the heavens after making the ultimate sacrifice for our sin in order to enter the Throne Room of God. Here, Jesus would sit at God's right hand, with the express purpose of interceding for you and me before God. Unlike the priest of the Old Testament, Jesus never leaves God's presence in heaven.

Another very significant difference between Jesus and the Old Testament high priest is in His title. The high priest of antiquity was a mere shadow of the ultimate priest who would come in the person of Jesus. The human priest performed the duties prescribed by God, but the atonement was limited. No priest was ever called the Son of God. Only Jesus, the only begotten of the Father, full of grace and truth, was called the Son of God. Because Jesus is the Son of God, we can rest confidently in a completed atonement of our sin.

We do not have a high priest who is unable to sympathize with our weaknesses, but we have one who has been tempted in every way, just as we are—yet was without sin. Hebrews 4:15

I think this place of differentiation between Jesus and the earthly high priest is glaringly obvious! What about you?

What does this verse say about Jesus' temptation to sin?

_____

_____

_____

_____

Based on what you know about Jesus' life, list a few temptations He might have encountered.

_____

_____

_____

_____

What does this verse say is different about Jesus with regard to temptation and sin?

_____

_____

_____

_____

As I think about Jesus being my Great High Priest, I am so thankful that He knows what I go through on a daily basis. Jesus understands the temptations I face: temptation to lose my temper, overeat, be prideful, lie, and all sorts of other things. Jesus faced all these temptations as a Man who walked this earth, yet He did not sin. I don't know about you, but I am much more likely to trust someone who I know has walked the same path I walk than another person who has no idea what my life is like.

I'm reminded of **2 Corinthians 1:3-5 (NIV1984)**. These verses are speaking specifically of the troubles we face as we walk the dusty sod of earth but can be applied to our temptations as well.

 Fill in the blanks: *Praise be to the God and Father of our Lord _____*
Christ, the Father of all compassion and the God of all comfort, who
_____ us in all our troubles, so that we can
comfort _____   _____   _____
_____ with the comfort we ourselves have received from God.
For just as the _____ of Christ flow over into our
lives, so also through Christ our comfort _____.

Do you see the correlation? Jesus was tempted, so He could understand our temptations and provide us with strength and overcoming power. Now that is something to get excited about! You and I do not have to fight the temptations

Satan throws at us alone. Jesus sees, knows, and understands what we deal with, and He is right beside us, ready to help us resist just as He resisted.

Jesus truly is the BETTER High Priest! At this very moment, He sits just to the right of God, talking to His Father about YOU! Listen closely and you will hear those words of love He speaks to the Father about you. He loves you so!

MEDITATION MOMENT:

In what area of your life do you need the overcoming power and strength of Jesus to help you resist temptation and walk out your life and legacy well? Take some time to journal about it here, being careful about using names if it would be hurtful to another person.

Write out a personal prayer to Jesus and ask Him to be your Great High Priest in every way you listed as we began this day of study.

Day 5 – What's the Big Deal About a Better Priest?

As children we often said to one another things like "My daddy's bigger than your daddy" or other comparison statements designed to degrade the other person's possession. Even as adults, we can fall into this trap. Consider the bumper stickers that were popular a few years ago—"My honor roll student is smarter than your football player," or even "My child is on the honor roll at High Brow Elementary"—comparison statements designed to elevate one and denigrate another.

On our final day of study this week, we have the opportunity to make one of these comparison statements in a positive way. The New Testament High Priest, Jesus, is BETTER than the Old Testament high priest. I hope we have established this as a point of fact in your mind and heart. Oh, I know there are those who will disagree with me. Our precious Jewish friends who do not agree with us that Jesus is Messiah are still waiting for the day when the third temple will be built on the Temple Mount in Jerusalem and the daily sacrifices resume. I long for Jewish people to recognize Jesus as Messiah. God instructed us in Psalm 122:6 to "pray for the peace of Jerusalem." True peace in Jerusalem will not be found in land-for-peace deals. True peace in Jerusalem will be found only in recognizing Jesus as King of Kings and Lord of Lords.

Will you turn with me to Hebrews 7? In the final verses of this chapter, I want to focus on one verse that cements in stone the assertion that Jesus is the better priest. Please read **Hebrews 5:1-11 and 7:20-28** for context.

Please list the things about Jesus from this group of verses that make Him a BETTER priest.

_____

_____

_____

Today I want us to focus on the eternality of Jesus as one of the key ingredients to His BETTER priesthood. Although there were several things that made Jesus a BETTER priest, Hebrews 7:25 offers Jesus' eternal nature as being of prime importance. The study notes in my *NLT Study Bible – New Living Translation* say the following about verse 25:

> "Since Jesus lives forever, the salvation he brings also lasts forever. To draw near to an eternal God, we need an eternal priest."

God established the priesthood in the Old Testament as a way for the people to draw near to Him. The Old Testament priesthood was flawed by the mortality of the priests, among other things. In order for permanent, complete, and eternal reconciliation to occur between God and man, there had to be a BETTER priest, an eternal priest who could, once and for all, offer a sacrifice that would bring reconciliation between God and all people. Jesus fit the bill perfectly.

Please write **Hebrews 7:25** in the space provided below.

_____

_____

_____

_____

To write this day's lesson, I had at least three translations of the Bible before me. Honestly, I love the way each of them renders verse 25. This verse is really the Gospel in a nutshell. Let's dig into it for the remainder of this lesson

In each translation, the very first word of verse 25 is "therefore." When you see the word *therefore* in the Bible, you need to ask the question, what is the word *therefore* there for? Typically, *therefore* points the reader back to the previous passage, and that is the case with this *therefore*. This verse reminds us that the writer was just discussing the old priesthood and the need for a BETTER one.

"Therefore he is *able*." Stop the presses! Halt! We need to look at the word *able* because it is a four-letter word that packs an incredible punch. In the Greek, the word is *dynamai*. Does that word look familiar to you?

What English word do you find in *dynamai*?

_____

If you said dynamite, you get a gold star!!! Dynamite has incredible power and is a force to be reckoned with. It needs only to be put to use, and it accomplishes the task of destruction. Consider the definition of *dynamai*: "To be able, have power to do something by virtue of one's own ability and resources; to be sufficiently powerful." [22] Now let's re-word the beginning of verse 25 using this definition and see what we get.

"Therefore he (Jesus) has the power to do something by virtue of his own ability and resources…."

"Therefore he (Jesus) is sufficiently powerful…."

So, since there was a need for a new and improved priesthood, the one who has the power to be that eternal priest by virtue of his own ability and resources can do the job.

Let's review for a moment. Jesus has the power to be that eternal priest by virtue of his own ability and resources. List the unique abilities and resources Jesus has that enable Him to be that eternal priest. Go back to our earlier readings in Hebrews 5 and 7 to find these.

_____

_____

_____

_____

Jesus is the BETTER priest because He, the Son of God, is sufficiently powerful. No human priest was eternal, holy, and undefiled. He offered the perfect sacrifice in order to open the way of access to God. Only Jesus, the BETTER priest, could do these things.

"Therefore he is able to save *completely*." Other words or phrases used for *completely* are *once and forever* or *to the uttermost*. The Greek word used for *completely* is only used one other time in the entire Bible. Let's take a look at it very quickly.

Turn to **Luke 13:11** and see if you can find a word that means the same thing as *completely* or *to the uttermost*.

_____

This one is a little tricky. Did you find it? If you are reading from the New International Version the words you are looking for are *at all*, while in the New King James the words are *in no way*. The woman Jesus was interacting with had a back that was so bent and deformed she could not stand up straight at all. She could not straighten up *to the uttermost*. Her posture was so disfigured it was impossible for her to look anyone in the eye, except for a small child.

I have never had back problems, but I know many people who do, and they are truly debilitated. There is a precious older couple in our church, and the lady has chronic back problems. Several years ago she had spinal surgery to insert rods in her back because osteoporosis had basically destroyed her spinal column. The surgery went well, but a few years later the rods broke. Now, she is bent over and is unable to straighten up completely. She walks with her face toward

the floor, yet I've never once heard her complain about her predicament. She and her husband still travel for pleasure, despite the pain she experiences on a daily basis.

As I think about this lady in my church and the Luke 13:11 woman, I see a comparison to how bent and broken we can become because of sin in our hearts. When we allow our hearts to be enticed by sin, almost before we know it, Satan has nearly broken our backs with it. In what seems like the blink of an eye, we can be so bent over and consumed by sin that we think we will never be able to walk upright in holiness again.

May I give you some very good news? *Therefore he [Jesus] is able to save completely those who come to God through Him, because He always lives to make intercession for them* **(Hebrews 7:25, NKJV)**. You are never too bent or too broken that Jesus cannot bring healing to your life and heart. NEVER! Trust me. If it were possible to be so broken and bent that Jesus was powerless to help, I would have been that person. Jesus said, *I have come that they may have life, and have it more abundantly* **(John 10:10, NKJV)**. When we submit to the touch of the Great Physician, our sin is forgiven, and we are able to walk completely upright in holiness.

MEDITATION MOMENT:

Is there sin in your life that is causing you to be bent and broken? Do you long to walk in holiness to the uttermost? Jesus is able to bring forgiveness and healing to your life and heart if you will allow Him. Right now, in the space below, name the sin(s) that has you bent and broken. Voice to Jesus your desire to be free from that sin. Ask Him to forgive you for allowing it into your life. Open wide your arms, and continue praying the following prayer (or one similar to it) and offer your entire being to the Lord.

> *Dear God,*
>
> *I present my body, heart, and mind to You as a living sacrifice. I want it to be holy and acceptable to You because that is the only place I will find true freedom in this life. Give me a heart that desires to please only You, Lord. Consume me from the inside out and use me to show others who are bent with sin Your love, grace, and mercy. Help me walk in holiness from this day forth. In the strong and overcoming name of Jesus, I ask these prayers. Amen.*

May I Serve You?

I may be one of the few women in the known world who is not a chocoholic. I know, I'm weird. I don't dislike chocolate, I simply prefer other flavors. I figured, though, that I needed to include at least one recipe for a chocolate dessert to appease my chocoholic friends.

This week's dessert recipe is pulled from the archives of my mother's recipe book. This chocolate sheet cake she has made for decades combines gooey, chocolaty cake with rich chocolate frosting. For the chocolate lover, it is lick-your-fingers goodness. Personally, I would accompany this with a tall, cold glass of milk. For those who prefer coffee, brew yourself a cup of Newman's Special Blend Extra Bold® Coffee. I hope you enjoy it.

RECIPE

Barbara's Chocolate Sheet Cake

2 cups sugar
2 cups cake flour
1 stick margarine
1 cup water
3 ½ tablespoons cocoa

½ cup shortening
½ cup buttermilk
1 teaspoon vanilla flavoring
1 teaspoon baking soda
2 eggs, beaten

Preheat over to 400° F. Melt margarine, water, cocoa, and shortening in saucepan. Place sugar and flour in mixer and add the melted ingredients. Mix well. Add buttermilk, vanilla, soda, and beaten eggs to ingredients in mixer and beat well. Grease and flour a large sheet pan. Pour batter into sheet pan. Bake for 20 minutes. Leave in pan to frost and serve.

RECIPE

FROSTING

1 stick margarine
3 ½ tablespoons cocoa
5 tablespoons milk

1 box powdered sugar, sifted
1 teaspoonful vanilla
Pecans, if desired

Melt margarine in heavy saucepan. Add cocoa and milk. Remove from heat. Add powdered sugar and vanilla. If frosting is too thick, add a few drops of milk. Garnish with pecans if desired.

Week 3 – A Better Covenant – The New Blend

Covenant. It sounds like such an old-fashioned word, doesn't it? No one really uses it anymore, do they? Could it be that the word covenant is not used any longer because we don't understand it? Perhaps it is not used very often because it is a concept that requires commitment, courage, and holiness.

In our modern world, most people simply don't understand the concept of covenant. Neither did I until I did a Bible study about the topic. Several years ago, my small group did Kay Arthur's incredible study entitled *Covenant*. We were blown away. All of us are mature Christians…both spiritually and physically, yet few of us truly understood the importance that God places on covenants in the Bible. As we studied the key covenants in Scripture, we gained a clearer understanding of what a covenant is and how deadly serious God is about covenant keeping. The study literally took me to my knees before God.

In the past year or so, I've had the opportunity to share on the covenant topic with a few groups. Without exception, the eyes of the audience are opened and their hearts are taken to a new level of commitment to the Lord as a result.

This week, in our journey through Hebrews, we will learn about the importance of covenant. We will discover that Jesus is the mediator of a new and better covenant directed at those who are willing to accept Him as Lord and Savior. There is as much difference in the Old and New Covenants as there is in stone and flesh. Let's get started.

Day 1 – A Glance Back at the Old

Is it me, or does anyone else feel that the quality of television programming has declined hugely? Perhaps that is why I love re-runs.

Recently I was speaking out of town and arrived at my hotel in the afternoon. After doing a bit of work on the message I was to bring the next day, I ordered room service and settled in to do something I rarely do. I began channel surfing to find something to watch for an hour or so. After a few minutes of flipping channels, I settled on re-runs of M*A*S*H. This has long been one of my very favorite television programs, and I seldom take time to watch it. The characters were intriguing and the dialogue was just plain funny. Captains Pierce and Honeycutt were always into some sort of mischief, which usually involved causing great angst to Majors Burns and Houlihan. Then, there was the extremely colorful Corporal Klinger, who consistently tried to get a discharge from the military on the grounds that he was crazy. Cross-dressing was a favorite tactic of Klinger's to try and convince Colonel Potter to send him stateside for a permanent visit. Who can forget tender-hearted Radar O'Reilly, the young kid who kept the M*A*S*H unit running and on occasion, aided and abetted Captains Pierce and Honeycutt in one of their hair-brained schemes.

In the motel room that day, I watched two hours of M*A*S*H re-runs and laughed out loud time and time again. Sometimes it is good to take a look back at the old in order to get a better perspective on the new. That is precisely what we are going to do today in our Bible study time.

As we enter a new week of studying the better things of the book of Hebrews, we come to the topic of covenant. What a crucial topic, yet it is one that most Christians do not understand. I offer a two-hour class on covenant, and most who go through it are surprised at the importance of this topic to the Lord. Today we will dig way back into the Old Testament to review the finer details of the Old Covenant, also called the Mosaic Covenant, so we can ultimately understand why a new and better Covenant was needed.

Let's begin by defining the term *Old Covenant*. In your own words, explain what you believe is meant by the term *Old Covenant*.

_____

_____

_____

In **Exodus 34:28**, we will discover if you were correct in your definition of *Old Covenant*. Specifically, what does this verse say the *Old Covenant* consists of?

_____

_____

_____

In our culture today, we do not fully understand the word *covenant*. We understand contract, but covenant is very different. The Hebrew word used for *covenant* in the Bible is *beriyt*. Consider the definition of *beriyt*: "denotes a treaty between nations, a covenant between individuals or friends, a compact between a monarch and his subjects, or a marriage covenant between husband and wife; often accompanied by signs, sacrifices, and a solemn oath which sealed the relationship with promises of blessing for obedience and curses for disobedience. The ancient custom of ratifying solemn covenants involved passing between the divided parts of a sacrifice." [23]

As we look at the Old Covenant, or the Mosaic Covenant, and compare it with the New Covenant, I hope you will begin to see this definition come alive. The Old Covenant was indeed a compact between a monarch (God) and his subjects (Israel). There were promises of blessing for obedience and curses for disobedience.

In the span of three months, Moses had brought the children of Israel out of slavery in Egypt and to the base of Mount Sinai where they camped. These chosen people had seen God conquer their enemies in three-dimensional Hollywood fashion. They had been given manna to eat and bitter water-made-drinkable by God. He had fully provided for them in every way possible. Now, the people had to decide if they would follow whole-heartedly this God of Abraham, Isaac, and Jacob, and enter into covenant with Him. God was fully prepared to be their God if they would commit to obedience to His will and way. Let's take a look at God's words to the Israelites through Moses. There are two passages that I don't want you to miss.

First go to **Exodus 19:4-6 (NIV1984)** and fill in the blanks:

You yourselves have seen what I did to _____,
and how I _____ _____ you on ea-
gles' wings and brought you to _____.
Now if you obey me _____and keep my
_____, then out of all nations you will be my
_____ _____. Although the whole earth is

mine, you will be for me a kingdom of_____ and
a _____ nation.

Did you note God's heart for this people showing through His words to them? I can almost hear the music swelling as He reminds them of all He has done for them. Huge things. God's love for the Israelites caused Him to do mighty miracles for them. All He asks is their allegiance and obedience. Does it tug at your heartstrings? Soften your heart? Does it sound familiar? It should. In 1 Peter 2:9 we read something similar.

Go to **1 Peter 2:9** and write in the space below the words you find that are similar to these in Exodus.

_____

_____

_____

In Exodus, God is speaking to the physical Israel. In 1 Peter, God speaks to the church of Jesus Christ. What He offered Israel in Exodus, He now offers you and me—all in exchange for our allegiance and obedience to Him—a kingdom of priests and a holy nation. Israel could have been obedient by yielding their hearts to God who dwelt among them. You and I can do it because of God's Spirit dwelling within us. God does not ask us for obedience and then walk off and say, "Now figure out how to do it." No, He asks us for obedience and then gives us the Spirit to enable us to do it. What a deal! We just have to do it.

In the next passage God speaks to the Israelites of blessings for obedience and curses for disobedience.

Look up the following verses in Deuteronomy and note whether God is speaking of a blessing for obedience or a curse for disobedience and what the blessing or curse would be.

Deuteronomy 11:8–9

_____

_____

_____

Deuteronomy 11:13–15

_____

_____

_____

Deuteronomy 11:16–17

_____

_____

_____

Deuteronomy 11:18–21

_____

_____

_____

Deuteronomy 11:22–23

_____

_____

_____

The Old Covenant was a conditional covenant. God promised Israel certain things IF they were obedient to His commands. At the same time, God was crystal clear about the consequences of disobedience. God did not set out these commands because He had an ego problem. God always acts out of love toward His children. He knew what would be best for the children of Israel, if they did what He told them to do.

I wish I could tell you they were always obedient, but they were not. They paid a very high price for their disobedience over the decades. Death, defeat, and ultimately, captivity resulted from their refusal to obey God's commands. Four hundred years before the birth of Christ, the nation of Israel had been split in two and both nations were carried off into captivity: Israel by the Assyrians, and Judah by the Babylonians.

I sure am glad you and I are not like those rebellious Israelites, aren't you? I'm sure we never disobey God…do we? Unfortunately, most of us resemble the Israelites more than we care to admit. God says, "Do not lie," and what do we do?

We tell lies. God commands us to abstain from sexual immorality, yet we think it is our prerogative to "do what feels good and makes us happy." Why can't we get it through our heads that God's commands are for our good? Just as a parent knows what is best for her child, God knows what is best for us. He desires to bless us, yet because He is a just God, He will not bless our disobedience. He *cannot* bless our disobedience. We can either do this thing called life our way and deal with the consequences that come by thinking we know best. Or, we can do it God's way and experience the blessing of walking in obedience. I don't know about you, but I would much rather have blessings than unpleasant consequences.

Before we finish today, let's do one more thing. This exercise will transition us into our study tomorrow.

Write out the Ten Commandments (Exodus 20:1-17) in the space below. Although you may know them from memory, please use your Bible and write them word for word. Speak them out loud as you write them. There is power when the Word of God is spoken aloud.

_____

_____

_____

_____

_____

_____

_____

_____

MEDITATION MOMENT:

Now that we have studied about the priesthood, share what it means to you to be a kingdom of priests and a holy nation. What does that look like in your own life and walk with Christ?

Day 2 – Why Did We Need A Better Covenant?

My friend, Cindy, tells the story of an incident that occurred when her children were small. Both of them had done something they knew was wrong and had been caught red-handed in the act. Their father, Robert, looked at them with that look only a Daddy can give and told them they had two choices as punishment. The first was to go to their room and the second was a spanking. Immediately, Caitlin went flying to her room, wisely choosing the less severe of the two punishments. Manning, who was younger than Caitlin, looked Robert squarely in the eye and said, "Well, spank me then."

In this story we find the reason the Israelites needed a BETTER Covenant. Young Manning knew the rules and knew when he had done wrong; however, just being caught and punished was not enough to change his heart and make him want to do better. The Israelites knew the law, as well as the punishment for breaking the law, but it was not enough to bring about a heart change for them. The Old Covenant not only consisted of the Ten Commandments, but also dozens of other rules and requirements. It was incumbent upon an observant person to know these laws and adhere strictly to them. Let's take a look at some of the laws and the consequences for breaking them in an effort to get a clearer picture of how the Israelites were to live.

I am going to give you a Scripture reference from the Old Covenant/Law, and I want you to note what the rule/law was and any consequence for breaking the law.

Exodus 21:2 _____

Exodus 21:12-14 _____

Exodus 22:20 _____

Leviticus 5:2-6 _____

Leviticus 20:1-2 _____

Leviticus 20:9 _____

Leviticus 20:10 _____

Leviticus 26:14-17 _____

Do you see how very specific God was with the Israelites, and still they were disobedient? Not even the threat of horrible punishment was enough to deter some of them from their rebellion.

God gave the Israelites laws to govern every aspect of their lives. If you can imagine a scenario, there was a law pertaining to it. There were even laws for scenarios that would never have occurred to you and me. Let's take a look at more of the rules under which the average Israelite had to live.

Match the rule/law with the verse in which it is found.

_____ Leviticus 11:1-3   A. Law concerning plowing a field

_____ Leviticus 12:2   B. Law concerning cooking baby goats

_____ Leviticus 13:29-30   C. Law concerning which
                                                                        animals could be eaten

_____ Leviticus 15:18   D. Law concerning bodily
                                                                        discharges and sexual intimacy

_____ Leviticus 19:32   E. Law for women who bear male children

_____ Leviticus 25:35-37   F. Law concerning the consequences
                                                                        of a woman intervening
                                                                        in a fight between two men

_____ Deuteronomy 14:21   G. Law concerning sores
                                                                        on the head or beard

_____ Deuteronomy 22:10   H. Law concerning lending to the poor

_____ Deuteronomy 25:11-12   I. Law concerning the elderly

Didn't I tell you there were laws concerning every aspect of the Israelite life? We could study for days and not cover all the laws the Lord gave the Israelites. There were so many laws they became exceedingly restrictive, which was exactly why God gave them. A Jewish man would have to spend his entire day trying not to break a law. Even today, Orthodox Jews are incredibly weighed down by the restrictive laws of Judaism.

Consider the Shabbat elevator. Jewish law prohibits any type of work on the Sabbath, which begins at sundown on Friday and ends at sundown on Saturday.

Even the operating of electric switches is prohibited. The Shabbat elevator is programmed to allow the Jews to ride the elevator without having to press a button to indicate which floor of a building they need to stop on. The elevator may be programmed to stop at every floor, stop at alternating floors, or go all the way to the top of the building and stop only while it is descending. In a building without a Shabbat elevator, non-Jews are hired to press the elevator buttons in order to prevent Jewish people from breaking the Sabbath by performing work.

The Old Covenant was so burdensome it was impossible to be fully justified in the eyes of God simply by keeping the law. God knew this. He knew no man could fully keep the Old Covenant in order to gain right standing with God.

Write out **Romans 5:20** in the space below.

_____

_____

_____

_____

_____

God's purpose in giving the Old Covenant law was to bring people to the realization that they could not do enough good works or avoid enough bad actions to gain righteousness before God. God wanted man to seek a BETTER way, and that way was by grace through faith in Jesus Christ. The entire seventh chapter of Romans deals with the tension between the law and sin.

In **Romans 7:7** Paul tells us that the law taught him something. What did the Old Covenant law teach about God's creation?

_____

_____

_____

_____

Once people learned the do's and don'ts of the law, what happened then, according to **Romans 7:8**?

_____

_____

_____

Consider a small child. She or he does something her or his parent does not want her or him to do. The parent scolds her or him and tells him or her not to do it again. A typical child will not say, "Oh, that is bad for me and I won't do it again." No, she or he will try it again and again, just to see if he or she can get away with it. She or he continues to be disobedient until the punishment becomes severe enough to deter him or her. This is precisely what Paul is talking about in **Romans 7:15-20**. Sin causes us to do what we know we should not do, and not to do what we know we should do. In a cry of utter frustration, Paul says in verse 24: _O wretched man that I am! Who will deliver me from this body of death?_ He quickly answers his own question with a shout of praise to God in verse 25: _I thank God—through Jesus Christ our Lord!_

Paul recognizes that it is only through faith in Jesus Christ and through the indwelling Spirit of God living in us that we can be victorious over sin. No amount of law keeping will bring victory in this area.

You, my friend, will never be good enough to obtain right standing before God. Neither will I. It is only when we accept Jesus as our Lord and Best Friend that we are given right standing before God. Praise Jesus for the New Covenant in His blood. Tomorrow we will look more at this New Covenant.

MEDITATION MOMENT:

Journal about a time when you did what you did not want to do _OR_ you did not do what you knew you should do. If you have not asked God to forgive you for those actions, spend time in prayer doing that now. Thank God that because of the blood of Jesus, you stand clean and righteous before Him.

Day 3 – A Visit with Jeremiah

I am a total sucker for a great action-packed novel. You know, one of those where you cannot, for the life of you, figure out the next twist or turn in the plot, and the situations and characters are so real you find yourself thinking about them long after you have completed the book. In your mind, they might live next door to you or work in the building down the block. Although you always go to bed by 10:00 P.M., you find yourself still awake and reading long after midnight. You just cannot put the book down.

Several years ago, I found a series of novels by Joel Rosenberg that fit this "cannot put the book down" category. You know, books that will not let you focus on laundry, dirty dishes, mopping, or anything else until they are read. The Rosenberg books are thrilling, gripping stories that seem to be ripped right out of the pages of today's newspapers. What makes them even more intriguing is the fact that they are based on a portion of the biblical book of Ezekiel—chapters 38 and 39 to be exact.

I read the first two books on my trip to Israel in 2006. On the flight over, I read *The Last Jihad*, while the flight back found me reading *The Last Days*. I happened to be traveling with a group from my church on that trip, and my pastor thought I was crazy for taking a book entitled *The Last Jihad* into Israel. He was convinced they would be leaving me in an Israeli prison. Teeheehee! Guess who read *The Last Jihad* on the plane ride back from Israel? Yep, my pastor. He was totally drawn into the plot and characters of Rosenberg's books.

Joel Rosenberg has been hailed as a modern-day Nostradamus because events written about in his books came true in the days after the books were released. For example, *The Last Jihad*, written nine months before the September 11th terror tragedies in New York and Washington, DC, told of hijacked airplanes on a kamikaze mission into an American city. Sound familiar? *The Last Days* has the lead characters in the middle of a massive explosion in Gaza and the West Bank. In just a few pages, the leader of the Palestinian Authority, Yassar Arafat, is dead and Islamic radicals attempt to take over the West Bank. Again, *The Last Days* was written months prior to Arafat's November 2004 death and Hamas' 2007 takeover of the Gaza Strip.

Can Rosenberg foretell the future? I'm not sure about that; however, the Bible gives us a pretty clear picture of what the last days will look like, and strangely enough, they look an awful lot like the days in which we live.

The prophet Jeremiah might have been a relative of Joel Rosenberg's because he certainly prophesied about a cataclysmic event that would happen hundreds of years in the future. Let's read about it in **Jeremiah 31:31-34 (NIV1984).**

> *The time is coming, declares the LORD, when I will make a new covenant with the house of Israel and with the house of Judah. It will not be like the covenant I made with their forefathers when I took them by the hand to lead them out of Egypt, because they broke my covenant, though I was a husband to them, declares the LORD. This is the covenant I will make with the house of Israel after that time, declares the LORD. I will put my law in their minds and write it on their hearts. I will be their God, and they will be my people. No longer will a man teach his neighbor, or a man his brother, saying, 'Know the LORD,' because they will all know me, from the least of them to the greatest, declares the LORD. For I will forgive their wickedness and will remember their sin no more.*

Now that you have read the Jeremiah passage, please go back and highlight or circle every reference to *covenant* that you find.

How many *covenants* are being referenced in these verses?
Circle the correct answer: ONE   TWO   THREE   TEN

God says He will make a NEW COVENANT. With whom will He make this covenant?

_____

The Old Covenant made at Mount Sinai between God and Moses and the Israelites was written on tablets of stone. On what does God say this NEW COVENANT will be written?

_____

If this NEW COVENANT is made with Israel, given what you know about the Jewish people, does the NEW COVENANT pertain to modern day Israel? If it does, are they embracing it? Why or why not?

_____

_____

_____

Let's take these four verses apart and see what we learn about this New Covenant. Glance back at verse 31. In this verse, we find extremely significant wording when God says He will make a new covenant. The Hebrew word used for make is *karat*. Not, karat, as in diamonds, but *karat*, as in "to cut, cut off, to make a covenant." This word is used "to denote making (literally, 'cutting') a covenant, because animals had to be killed in order to ratify the agreement." [24]

In order to understand why making this New Covenant is such a big deal, we must understand the importance of covenants in general.

Do you remember from a few days ago that the Hebrew word for covenant is *beriyt?* It means "a treaty between nations, a covenant between individuals or friends, a compact between a monarch and his subjects, a marriage covenant between husband and wife. A covenant was a contract often accompanied by signs, sacrifices, and a solemn oath which sealed the relationship with promises of blessing for obedience and curses for disobedience." Can you sense the seriousness of a covenant? Consider the final part: "The ancient custom of ratifying solemn covenants involved passing between the divided parts of a sacrifice." [25]

In our American culture we do not have a frame of reference for the concept of making a covenant. The Israelites would have immediately understood exactly what God was saying. To understand the significance of making a covenant, let's look at a covenant made by God with Israel.

Please turn to **Genesis 15,** read the entire chapter, and answer the following questions.

We read in this chapter of a discussion between God and whom?

_____

_____

What is Abram's complaint against God in verse 2?

_____

_____

How did God answer Abram's complaint in verse 5?

_____

_____

Look once again at the definitions of the words *karat* and *beriyt*.

What usually happened to bring about the ratification of a covenant?

_____

_____

Jump back to **Genesis 15:9-10**. What happened in these verses?

_____

_____

_____

Now, look at **Genesis 15:17-21**. In these verses the presence of God, as represented by a smoking firepot and a blazing torch, passed between the divided parts of the sacrifice Abram had set up. In this moment, God cut covenant with Abram and his descendants.

In your own words, describe the covenant God made with Abram. What did God promise to Abram?

_____

_____

_____

_____

_____

God promised Abram and his descendants a land they could call their own. Did God keep His covenant with Abram? Did Abram's descendants possess a land given to them by God?

You have been so patient and diligent in your study today, but there is one more place we must go in order to answer those last two questions. Turn to Joshua 1 and read verses 1 through 5. Does any of this sound familiar given what you just read in Genesis 15? I think so. In these five verses God is giving Joshua final instructions before he leads the Israelites across the Jordan River and into the Promised Land. Promised. Land. What did God promise to Abram in the covenant He cut in Genesis 15? That's right! A land to call their own. Hundreds of years later, God fulfills the promise He made to Abram and the Israelites. Under the leadership of Joshua, they possessed the land of promise. Over the course of hundreds of additional years, the Israelites would lose their land because of

their worship of other gods; yet the One True God never completely removed Israel from their land.

God kept His covenant with Abram, because He is a covenant-keeping God. Covenants are very important to God, and He expects us to keep the covenants we make just as He keeps His. Tomorrow we will finish our visit with Jeremiah.

MEDITATION MOMENT:

If God is serious about covenant keeping, we should be as well. Consider any covenants you have made. I know we don't make covenants very often in our culture, but if you are married, you made a covenant with your spouse before God. God expects us to honor our marriage covenants. How are you doing at keeping your marriage covenant?

Day 4 – What about the Ten Commandments?

I love the New Year's holiday—a fresh start. A fun, new calendar with blank spaces for all that a fresh year will bring. My kitchen is enveloped in the smells of collard greens, black-eye peas, and cornbread. The new year ushers in the quiet days of winter without all the hustle and bustle of November and December. Soon, my Tuesday Bible study group and I will be back together studying God's Word. The newness of the year holds so much promise and hope.

Although the New Year is what consumes each of us in January, the "old year" can still offer so much. Memories of the previous year can be tucked into the file drawers of my mind, only to be pulled out when needed. And trust me, they will be needed. So often it is only in reflecting back on the old that we get a solid grounding for the new. So it is with the Old and New Covenants. The freshness of the New Covenant does not render the Old Covenant useless.

What were Jesus' words concerning this very issue from **Matthew 5:17**? Note what He said here.

_____

_____

_____

I wanted you to see that passage before we take a look at Hebrews 8. This passage seems to be in direct opposition to Jesus' words in Matthew 5:17. We know that God's Word can be trusted. We also know that allowing Scripture to teach Scripture is the best way to understand the Bible. Let's dive into the Word and see if we can make sense of what seems to be contradictory. Remember, God is not the author of confusion, so there is an explanation for all this. We just have to dig to find it.

Read **Hebrews 8:7-13** and answer the following questions.

Verses 8-12 should be familiar to you from your study earlier in the week. What Old Testament passage is the author of Hebrews quoting?

_____

_____

_____

Twice in verse 13 the writer uses a bold word to describe what is happening to the Old Covenant. What is the word that was used?

_____

_____

_____

Here is where it seems that Scripture doesn't *gee-haw*, as my daddy used to say. That is Southern slang for "make sense" or "line up." If you have studied the Old Testament, you know that every jot and tittle of it points forward to Jesus Christ and the salvation He would offer on the cross. This is true for the Old Testament law, which includes the Ten Commandments.

• Fill in the blanks from **Romans 5:20** (NIV1984): *The _____ was added so that the _____ might increase. But where _____ increased, _____ increased all the more.*

What we find here is that the purpose of the law was to show the Jewish people they could not keep the law in its totality. Because no one is perfect, other than Jesus, everyone would end up breaking the law. Just like the story of the rich young ruler whose piety overshadowed his honesty in his conversation with Jesus, everyone broke the law at some point, whether they would admit it or not. God instituted the law knowing this. His purpose was to use the Law to point mankind to a BETTER way…the New Covenant way.

So, what about this talk in Hebrews of rendering the Old Covenant obsolete? Recall that God made the Old Covenant with the Israelites. In the latter half of Exodus 23, God tells the Israelites all He will do for them *if* they keep His commandments and His Law. In Exodus 24, the Covenant is affirmed, and all the Israelites promised to be obedient to all that the Lord had commanded. By the time we read Exodus 32, Aaron and the Israelites have broken their promise to God, and they are worshiping a golden calf. This would not be the last time the Israelites failed to keep their end of the covenant bargain. Over and over, throughout the rest of the Old Testament, the Israelites cycle in and out of rebellion toward God. Finally, God's patience wore thin. He allowed the Israelites to be taken into captivity because of their rebellion and disobedience.

Then, in the fullness of time, God sent His Son, Jesus, to institute a New Covenant—not one written on tablets of stone, but a covenant written on the hearts of men. The Old Covenant had three categories or parts: the moral law, the civil or judicial law, and the ceremonial or religious law. The religious law spoke specifically to Israel's worship in the tabernacle. If you study the Old Testament tabernacle, you know that every part and piece of it points forward to Jesus. Even the Old Covenant feasts pointed forward to Christ. When Jesus came to earth to institute the New Covenant, the ceremonial or religious law was no longer needed. The principles behind the law, however, still apply; principles such as love the Lord your God with all your heart and worship Him only.

The civil law of the Old Covenant pertained to the daily life of the Israelites: what they could and could not eat, when they could work, how they dealt with diseases and impurities, and how they dealt with crime or injustice. Jesus was the personification of God's justice and righteousness. In Micah 6:8 (NIV1984), God told us what He requires of every man, woman, and child when He said, *He has showed you, O man, what is good. And what does the Lord require of you? To act justly and to love mercy and to walk humbly with your God*. Jesus lived out Micah 6:8 for the world to see; therefore, the civil portion of the Old Covenant law was no longer necessary. Yet its principles of cleanliness, eating for good health, and treating others with justice and mercy are timeless and should guide our actions.

Finally, the moral law or the Ten Commandments required absolute obedience. It revealed God's nature and will for man. It is the very foundation of our nation's moral law and still requires obedience. Jesus kept the moral law perfectly, giving us His example to follow.

Consider this from *Word Biblical Commentary–Hebrews* concerning this matter of the Old Covenant becoming obsolete in the presence of the New Covenant.

> "The supersession of the Old Covenant was not due simply to the unfaithfulness of the people to the stipulations of the covenant. It occurred because a new unfolding of God's redemptive purpose had taken place, which called for new covenant action on the part of God. That God took the initiative in announcing his intention to establish a new covenant with Israel indicates that he fully intended the first covenant to be provisional. Thus God finds fault with the Mosaic covenant, and not simply with the people." [26]

Everything about the Old Covenant law was fulfilled in Jesus Christ. Once He came to earth, died on the cross, and rose again, there was no more need for the tabernacle or the daily sacrifice, because the perfect sacrifice had been made once for all. There was no need for a human priest to act as an intercessor between people and God, because the way into the throne room of God was opened. There was no need for a law written on tablets of stone, because now

the law of God would be written on the hearts of all people. The New Covenant accomplished what the Old Covenant never could.

When the book of Hebrews was written in approximately 68 AD, the Temple was still standing in Jerusalem, the priests were still serving, and the sacrifices were still in place. Jesus had been back in heaven with the Father for about 35 years. But very soon the Jewish people would see the literal fulfilling of the Old Covenant becoming obsolete. In 70 AD, Titus destroyed Jerusalem, as well as the magnificent Temple. Gone was the Temple, the altar, the priesthood, the sacrifices…the Old Covenant.

As we close today, please turn to **2 Corinthians 5:17**. In light of what we have studied today, my guess is this verse may take on new meaning. Write the verse below.

_____

_____

_____

MEDITATION MOMENT:

The Jewish people still do not understand that Jesus is the Messiah for whom they long and look. They mourn the destruction of the Temple and the ceasing of the daily sacrifice. They plan the future construction of the Third Temple in order to resume the sacrifice. My heart breaks for blindness to the true and living sacrifice, Jesus Christ. Please join me in praying for the hearts of the Jewish people to be opened to the truth of the gospel.

Dear God, Your people, Israel, did not recognize their Jewish Messiah. I ask You to soften their hearts and open their eyes to the truth of Who Jesus is. You commanded us to pray for peace. My plea is that the Jews come to know Jesus as Savior and Lord. Do whatever it takes, Lord, to open their eyes to the reality of Jesus as the Messiah. In the strong name of Jesus. Amen.

Day 5 — The New Covenant

You may be doing this Bible study in the winter, but as I write this day of study, I periodically gaze out my windows and see all kinds of new life. It is mid-March, early spring. Although spring has not officially sprung according to the calendar, Mother Nature begs to differ. Here in the South we have had an unusually warm winter, and the trees and flowers are blooming like crazy. Daffodils and forsythia color the world a beautiful bright yellow, while the Bradford pear trees add a milky white to nature's canvas. Very soon the dogwood blooms will burst forth, declaring that spring and Easter have arrived. Every kind of bird imaginable seems to have found its way to my feeder, and soon even the tiny hummingbirds will appear in our part of the country. Spring brings new life and new perspective with it.

Since I am in the mood to think about fresh, new things, I think today would be a fine day to wrap up our study of the New Covenant with an examination of just who the intended recipients of the New Covenant were. I'm in an adventurous mood, so let's take a walk down an oft-debated and sometimes confusing path.

Read **Hebrews 8:8-10** and note with whom the New Covenant would be made.

_____

_____

In **Luke 22:20** we find Jesus talking about the New Covenant. Write His words here.

_____

_____

_____

Who do you think is the "you" Jesus is referring to at the end of **Luke 22:20**? Who was sitting around the Passover table with Him that day?

_____

_____

_____

The New Covenant was made by God with the nation of Israel. Over the course of history from the time of Solomon until the time of Jesus, the Jewish people had repeatedly rejected God and been disobedient to His commands. Still, God promised them a do-over in Jeremiah 31. That do-over would be part of the New Covenant. In fact, they would have a couple of do-over opportunities.

When Jesus told the disciples in Luke 22:20 that His blood would be poured out for them, He was telling them the very essence of the New Covenant. He would be the ultimate Passover lamb, sacrificed for the sin of anyone who would receive Him. No other sacrifice would be necessary after He died and rose again. The New Covenant instituted by Christ would be written, not on tablets of stone, but in the hearts of the Jewish people. The key to the New Covenant for the Jewish people would be whether they accepted Jesus as that ultimate Passover lamb.

All four gospels tell us that the Jewish people not only rejected Jesus as the Messiah, they called for His death. And so, once again, the descendants of Abraham rejected God. Surely, this would be the final straw for God. He had taken them back time and again after cycles of rebellion and repentance. Surely, their rejection and killing of His Son, Jesus, would be what caused Him to reject them as His chosen people. No one would expect God to offer the Jews another opportunity. It would only be fair for God to say, "That's it. I've had it with you people. You've had your last chance. I'm done with you."

But as usual, God had a plan. Let's take a look at the plan. Read **Acts 13:42-47** and answer the following questions:

Who are the speakers in this passage?

_____

_____

To whom are they speaking?

_____

_____

Where did this interaction take place? What kind of building?

_____

_____

In your own words, summarize what Paul and Barnabas said to the audience in **Acts 13:46**.

_____

_____

_____

_____

When Paul and Barnabas told the audience that the Jews had rejected the Word of God, what they were really saying was that the Jews had rejected the provisions of the New Covenant. Because the Jews rejected the New Covenant, this offered Gentiles the opportunity to also receive eternal life.

This is where a hearty "Yippeee!" would be appropriate! Probably most of us would be considered Gentiles, although it would thrill me no end to think that a redeemed Jew is studying the Word with us. You and I have the opportunity to know Christ and be partakers of the New Covenant because the Jewish people rejected Jesus. Paul elaborates further on this in **Galatians 3:8, 14.** Take a moment and read those verses. Do you see how we, as Gentiles, are the fulfillment of the promise given to Abraham by God? We are the "all the nations." If that doesn't make you want to shout, I don't know what will.

So, where does that leave the Jewish people? Are they out in the cold, never to have another opportunity to come to know Jesus and have eternal life? Are you and I now God's chosen people? Here is where we enter highly disputed territory, but I believe it is worth a trip to the book of Romans to find our answer.

Read **Romans 11.** Yes, the entire chapter, and answer the following questions in order to discern where the Jewish people are in the great plan of God as of today:

Romans 11:1 asks a question and then gives the answer. Note the question and the answer here.

_____

_____

_____

_____

_____

We know that, as a whole, the nation of Israel rejected Jesus when He came the first time. **Romans 11:11** asks another question and then gives the answer. Note the question and the answer here.

_____

_____

_____

_____

_____

Also in **Romans 11:11** we are told that because the Jews rejected Jesus the first time, something key happened. What was it?

_____

_____

_____

_____

_____

The Apostle Paul, a Jew, is speaking to whom in this chapter? Hint: see **Romans 11:13.**

_____

_____

_____

_____

_____

In **Romans 11: 17** Paul seems to go off on a tangent and begins talking about trees. What kind of tree did he mention? Do you know the significance of this type of tree as it relates to Israel?

_____

_____

_____

_____

In **Jeremiah 11:16**, the nation of Israel is likened to an olive tree. Also in **Zechariah 4** the symbolism of the olive tree is applied to Israel. Paul uses this symbolism in **Romans 11:17** and following. In these verses he reminds the Gentiles that the olive tree (Israel) had branches broken off because of disobedience and unbelief. This gave opportunity for wild olive shoots (Gentiles) to be grafted into the parent tree. Our faith stands on the shoulders of our great Jewish ancestors like Abraham, Isaac, and Jacob. We are now part of the great lineage of faith passed down by the ancients.

Some scholars believe that the present day Church—a body of believers who have accepted Jesus as their Lord and Savior—has replaced Israel as God's chosen people. They claim that we are "spiritual Israel." I have a difficult time reconciling this point of view with Romans 11:1 and 11 that clearly say God has not rejected Israel.

> **Editors' Note:** Paul says in **Romans 2:28-29,** *A person is not a Jew who is one only outwardly, nor is circumcision merely outward and physical. No, a person is a Jew who is one inwardly; and circumcision is circumcision of the heart, by the Spirit, not by the written code.* So, all believers, who have placed their faith in Jesus, are the "spiritual Israel."

I love **Romans 11:22-24**. What does verse 23 tell us is the requirement for Israel to be grafted back into, or accepted into, God's kingdom?

Jewish people *must* place saving faith in Jesus Christ in order to be accepted back into God's kingdom. In **John 14:6 (NIV1984)** Jesus said, *I am the way and the truth and the life. No one comes to the father except through Me.* **No one** means **no one**…neither Jew nor Gentile can get to heaven without accepting Jesus as Lord and Messiah.

How does **Romans 11:25-26** further add to our understanding that the Jews can still accept God and be part of God's family along with the Gentiles?

_____

_____

_____

Let's finish this up. Fill in the blanks from **Romans 11:28 (NIV1984)**: *As far as the gospel is concerned, they are enemies on your account; but as far as election is concerned, they are _____ on account of the _____, for God's gifts and his _____ are _____.*

God did not call Israel as His chosen people and then discard them because they were disobedient. The Jewish people are still God's chosen people, and that choosing has its foundation in the very character of God. You and I, as Christians, have been granted entry into that chosen-ness because of **grace** and our belief in Jesus as Lord and Savior. Jews and Gentiles (Christians) have the same opportunity to receive Christ and experience salvation.

Meditation Moment:

Today I encourage you to pray for Jewish people who do not believe in Jesus. Ask the Lord to soften their hearts toward the Gospel. Many wonderful organizations actively minister and witness to Jewish people. Pray for the Word to penetrate their minds and hearts so they come to a place where they accept Jesus as their Jewish Messiah.

WEEK FOUR

May I Serve You?

I am crazy about coconut and will eat it in almost anything. I've never met a co-conut dessert I did not like, so there was no way I was leaving this recipe out of this Bible study. I got the recipe from my husband's cousin, Karen Lee. We have enjoyed it immensely over the years. In fact, when I have to take a dessert to a gathering, it is a safe bet that this pie will be my contribution.

You know what I like about it? Two things: it is incredibly rich and ridiculous-ly easy. Friend, it doesn't get any better than that. So, if you like coconut, you should plan for the ingredients for this pie to become staples in your pantry.

Because this dessert takes the meaning of RICH to a whole new level, I would recommend a smooth coffee such as Donut House® Light Roast Coffee.

RECIPE

Coconut Cheesecake Pie

8 ounce package cream cheese, softened

1 cup cream of coconut, stirred well (This can be found near the evaporated milk)

3.4-ounce package Jell-O® cheesecake instant pudding mix

7-10 ounces flaked coconut (Use the smaller amount for a smaller pie and the larger amount for a larger pie)

8-ounce container Cool Whip or other whipped topping

1 ready-to-use shortbread piecrust

Beat cream cheese and cream of coconut until smooth at me-dium speed with an electric mixer. Add pudding mix and beat until blended well. Stir in coconut, withholding about 4 table-spoons for garnish. Fold in whipped topping. Spread mixture evenly into crust. Toast 4 tablespoons of coconut and sprinkle on top of pie.

Cover and chill for at least 2-3 hours. Keep chilled and serve cold.

Week 4 – A Better Tabernacle – The Heavenly House Blend

Are you a fan of the Old Testament?

Odd question? Perhaps, but many people spend all their time reading and studying the New Testament without giving so much as a thought to the Old Testament. If God took the time to place Genesis through Malachi in the Scriptural canon, then it seems reasonable that He had a purpose for it. As you have already discovered, we are spending significant time in the Old Testament during this study of Hebrews. My secret hope is that you will come to love the Old Testament as much as I do.

There are many topics in the Bible that intrigue me, but few draw me in more than the wilderness tabernacle. It was not until I studied the Old Testament tabernacle in-depth that I truly understood the beauty and significance of it. Until I spent time learning about every part and piece of the structure, the portion of the Bible dealing with it was little more than ancient, and rather boring, history. Why in the world was so much ink wasted on describing a building? Little did I know that every part of the tabernacle pointed like a signpost to our Savior, Jesus Christ.

This week as we study Hebrews 9 we will unwrap the wonders that are the Old and New Covenant tabernacles. I pray you will be delighted by what you learn.

Day 1 – A Glance Back at the Old

As I think about this topic of the tabernacle, both in antiquity and the coming heavenly one, I am reminded of a story I read by Anne Ortlund in Charles Swindoll's book entitled *Swindoll's Ultimate Book of Illustrations and Quotes.*

> "When I was little we used to play church. We'd get chairs into rows, fight over who'd be preacher, vigorously lead the hymn singing, and generally have a great carnal time.

> "The aggressive kids naturally wanted to be up front, directing or preaching. The quieter ones were content to sit and be entertained by the up-fronters.

> "Occasionally we'd get mesmerized by a true sensationalistic crowd-swayer—like the girl who said, "Boo! I'm the Holy Ghost!" But in general, if the up-fronters were pretty good, they could hold their audience quite a while. If they weren't so good, eventually the kids would drift off to play something else—like jump rope or jacks.

> "Now that generation has grown up, but most of them haven't changed too much. Every Sunday they still play church. They line up in rows for the entertainment. If it's pretty good, their church may grow. If it's not too hot, eventually they'll drift off to play something else—like yachting or wife swapping." [27]

I fear our modern concept and attitude toward church has become twisted and very different from that which God intended. Today as we begin our look back at the Old Covenant tabernacle, we will hopefully begin to see the purpose for which God designed it. Let's do a bit of background research in order to attain a proper perspective of this very important structure.

Read **Genesis 2:15** and write out what took place in this verse.

_____

_____

Read **Genesis 3:8** and note what God was doing in this verse.

_____

_____

Finally, read **Genesis 3:22-24**. As punishment for man's disobedience and sin, God put man in a holy time-out. What did this entail?

_____

_____

_____

After God created man, there was perfect fellowship between them. They walked and talked together in the Garden of Eden. Once man chose disobedience toward God, that perfect fellowship was broken, and the consequence of this was that man was banished from the presence of God in the Garden of Eden. As a result, for hundreds and hundreds of years, man had no direct access to God. Now fast forward to Exodus 25. God has brought forth the nation of Israel from Abraham's descendants. Two million strong, they were captives in Egypt until God sent Moses to lead them out of captivity and into the land God promised Abraham. Never did the common person have a relationship with God.

But God had a plan to begin the restoration of fellowship between Him and His creation.

Turn to **Exodus 25:8** and write this verse below.

_____

_____

_____

_____

In **Exodus 25:9**, who would be the architect of this tabernacle?

_____

_____

What were God's instructions about the tabernacle in verse 9?

_____

_____

I know I am getting ahead of myself, but I cannot resist showing you something that thrills me every time I see it. Remembering God's instructions to Moses in Exodus 25:9, turn now to Hebrews 8.

Read **Hebrews 8:1-5** carefully note anything of significance regarding the tabernacle that you find written in both the Hebrews passage and the Exodus passage, focusing specifically on verse 5.

_____

_____

_____

_____

_____

Here we have the _pièce de résistance_. Look again at **Hebrews 8:5** (NIV1984) and fill in the blanks: _They serve at a sanctuary that is a _____ and _____ of what is in _____._

Are you excited yet? Do you see what I see? God had a reason for telling Moses to build the tabernacle exactly as He directed. It was not because God is a big ol' control freak and micro-manager. Rather, it was because the earthly tabernacle was a copy of a heavenly tabernacle. It was the earthly picture of a heavenly reality in which you and I will worship one day.

Oh mercy! I've just gone and given you the condensed version of our entire week of study. Now, what I want to do is take you through the specifics of this during our time together this week. Hang on! It is a wonderful ride.

Your assignment for the remainder of our day of study is to read **Exodus 26** and **Exodus 36:8-38**. Knowing this wilderness tabernacle is a copy of something in heaven, as you read these passages ask the Holy Spirit to begin to show you key words and phrases.

Note here any defining numbers you find as you read, the verse in which you find them, and what they correspond to. I'll give you an example to get you started:

Exodus 26:1 – Ten curtains

_____

_____

_____

_____

Note here color descriptions you find and the verse in which you find them. I'll give you an example to get you started:

Exodus 26:1 – Blue, purple, and scarlet yarn

_____

_____

_____

_____

Great work, my friend. Those are not simple passages to peruse, but God put them in the Bible for a reason, and we need to study them. Tomorrow we will build on what we learned in Scripture. Until then, I encourage you to ask the Lord to open your heart and mind to the beautiful concept we will be studying this week—the Tabernacle.

MEDITATION MOMENT:

Journal here about anything new you learned today concerning the tabernacle. Offer thanks to the Lord for illuminating your heart to the beauty of His Word.

_____

_____

_____

_____

_____

_____

_____

_____

_____

Day 2 – The Old Testament Tabernacle

Today, let's continue our lesson on the Old Testament tabernacle. Yesterday, we learned that the tabernacle built in the wilderness by Moses was a copy and shadow of something that exists in heaven. A copy is a reproduction, or a duplicate, of an original. With today's technologies, when we make copies of documents or pictures, we have something that is almost as clear and precise as the original. There will generally be some sort of defect or mark that lets you know you are looking at a copy and not the original document. A shadow is even less clear and precise. It is usually a darkened picture of something that is in the light; a hint or suggestion of something real. If we take these loose "Leah-definitions" of copy and shadow we find that the earthly tabernacle was a darkened picture of an original that is in the light—it was a hint or suggestion of something real.

Let's examine this structure and learn a bit about its significance. Turn back to Day 4 of Week 2 of our study and take a look at the layout of the Old Testament tabernacle. Mark that page so you can refer back to it over the course of this week.

You found in your reading yesterday that the temple was quite colorful with all the beautiful fabrics as well as the wood, gold, and bronze furnishings. It was also quite portable, so the Israelites could dismantle it whenever God instructed them to move to a new location. The tabernacle was rectangular-shaped and measured approximately 30 cubits long by 10 cubits wide, which would be 45 feet long by 15 feet wide. The opening, or front door, of the tabernacle faced east.

The tabernacle was divided into two main sections: the Most Holy Place and the Holy of Holies. In the Most Holy Place were three pieces of furniture. I want you to see them for yourself.

Read **Exodus 25:23–30** and describe (or draw, if you have an artistic bent) this first piece of furniture below.

Now, read **Exodus 25:31-39** and describe (or draw) this piece of furniture.

Finally, read **Exodus 30:8** and describe (or draw) this piece of furniture.

Can you imagine the beauty of this room? The Holy Place. Three articles of furniture, each covered with gold and illuminated by the light from the **lampstand**. Friend, there was more bling in this room than any of us have ever seen! It had to have been breathtaking to the priest when he entered each day to light the lamps.

On the north, or right hand side of the room, the **table of showbread** (or the bread of the presence), was positioned, while on the left, or south side of the room, sat the **lampstand**, which looked similar to a modern day menorah. Opposite the entrance, at the far end of the room just in front of the curtain that veiled the Holy of Holies, stood the **altar of incense** where the priest offered a burnt offering of incense twice a day.

Let's learn more about the significance of this room. It was to this room that the priest came twice a day to tend the lamps of the candlestick (or lampstand). There was no electricity in that day, so a wick inserted into olive oil produced light to illuminate the room. It is significant that the candlestick was made of pure gold and was highly ornate in its design. For the sake of space, we will forgo a discussion of the intricacies of the lampstand. What I do want to make sure you understand is the significance of the gold. Gold was, and still is, considered to be a precious metal. (Because of the rarity and purity of gold, scholars seem to believe that it represents the deity, or perfection, of Jesus.) In addition, Scripture tells us that the lampstand was fashioned of hammered, or beaten, gold.

Please look up **John 8:12 and John 9:5**. How did Jesus refer to Himself?

_____

_____

_____

Read **Mark 14:61-65**. What does verse 65 tell us the guards did to Jesus?

_____

_____

_____

Jesus, the Son of God, the God-Man, the Light of the World, was beaten beyond recognition prior to His crucifixion. Yet, even in death, He continued to shine forth the light from God that He had been sent to earth to offer to sinful man. The golden lampstand (or the candlestick), the only source of light for the Holy Place, pointed forward to the true Light that would come into the world hundreds of years later. It was a shadow of that which was to come.

Now, let's turn to the **table of showbread**.

According to **Exodus 25:23-24,** what two materials were used to make the table?

_____

_____

_____

We have already considered the significance of the gold. Let's turn now to the wood. Wood is a material that, while valuable for building purposes, eventually decays due to time and stress. Twelve cakes of bread, known as **Showbread** or the **Bread of the Presence**, were consistently present on the Table of Showbread for a whole week. Every Sabbath, new cakes were placed by the priests, who ate the old cakes in the Holy Place, the only place they could eat the bread—in the Lord's presence (See Leviticus 24:5-9.)

The Table that held the Bread of the Presence was evidence of the coming Messiah in amazing ways. The wood represented his human body, which would

eventually die after being tortured and crucified. The gold overlay represented, once again, his deity—He was God come to earth. The Bread of the Presence represented…well, I'll let you discover that for yourself.

Turn to **John 6:35** (NIV1984) and fill in the blanks: Then Jesus declared, *I am the* _____ *of* _____. *He who comes to me will never go* _____, *and he who believes in me will never be thirsty.*

Stunning, don't you think? The table that held the Bread of the Presence was a shadowy picture of Jesus and His earthly life work.

To be honest with you, my heart is overflowing right now. To see how God took the time and effort to show the gospel, eons before Jesus stepped foot on earth, tenders my heart. God cared about the eternal future of the people of OT times and, in essence, used the Tabernacle in the wilderness to preach the gospel to that generation. I've studied this many times, but it still amazes me every time. I love to study the Old Testament and see how beautifully it points toward the coming Christ. In truth, the Old Testament is all about Jesus…we simply must have ears to hear and eyes to see Him.

Finally, let's turn to the last piece of furniture in the Holy Place; the Altar of Incense. This piece was also made of wood overlaid with gold, once again pointing forward to the God-Man, Jesus Christ. The purpose of this altar was to burn incense before the Lord, as well as a yearly burnt offering. This was the closest piece of furniture in the Holy Place to the Holy of Holies where God's presence dwelled. Only once each year could the High Priest go beyond the Altar of Incense into the Holy of Holies.

What is the significance of burning incense in the tabernacle? To answer this question we must do more digging in God's Word. Look up the following verses and note the significance of incense in each.

Psalm 141:2

_____

_____

Revelation 5:8

_____

_____

Revelation 8:3-4

_____

_____

The incense is representative of the prayers of the saints—you and me—those who name Jesus as Lord over their life. The prayers of the saints speak of intercession before God. Remember that the golden altar, or altar of incense, was placed as deep into the Holy Place as it was possible to go. Beyond the veil that separated the Holy Place from the Holy of Holies was where God's presence dwelt. So, each morning and evening, the priest would enter the Holy Place and burn incense on the golden altar. The smell would waft upward and spread throughout the entire tabernacle, becoming a pleasing fragrance to God.

Stay with me. This is good stuff.

What does **Hebrews 7:25** tell us that Christ lives in heaven to do?

_____

_____

_____

You will recall from our second week of study that the Old Testament high priest was a forerunner of Jesus, the better High Priest, who lives in heaven to intercede before the throne of God for you and me. The altar of incense, representative of Christ because of the materials with which it was constructed, also speaks of His intercession before the Father for those who are His children. Once again, the picture is not vivid and clear, but rather a copy and shadow of what is in heaven. The prayers of the saints drift heavenward, and Jesus, the Great High Priest and Intercessor, pleads before the Father on our behalf.

I don't know about you, but I find great comfort in knowing that I don't always have to utter all the correct words in my prayers. All I need is a heart that cries out to God in utter dependence and trust. My Jesus, the One who intercedes for me before the throne of God, has all the right words. Praise You, Jesus!

I hope these two days of study about the Old Testament tabernacle have been as exciting for you as they have been for me. The tabernacle was a copy and shadow of a heavenly reality—one that awaits us in heaven and tomorrow in our study time.

MEDITATION MOMENT:

How has our study of the Old Testament tabernacle strengthened your faith? Does the fact that God so carefully detailed the tabernacle to point to Jesus Christ bless you? If God would take the time to work out the details of a building, how much more important are the details of your life to Him? God is intimately involved with every part of your life, whether you feel His presence or not. Use the space below to journal your thoughts and feelings about this fact.

Day 3 – Where God Dwelt

I do not have any skill or talent when it comes to decorating. Nope! I don't. In fact, I like to joke that my home is decorated in the modern redneck motif. We have dead animals hanging on many walls throughout our home, evidence of my man's fascination with hunting. If we could resurrect Marlin Perkins, we might even be able to host a segment of "Wild Kingdom" in our house.

In spite of my lack of decorating talent, I love to look at decorating magazines and watch HGTV's decorating and real estate programs. Strangely enough, I rarely attempt to replicate anything I see. The one time I did make an attempt at replicating a placement of books, it turned out nicely, but friends worried that I might have gone over the obsessive-compulsive edge. What did I do? I arranged one section of my bookshelves by color. All the books with blue spines were grouped together; all the books with red spines were grouped together, and on it went. I thought it turned out very well, and it does give the bookshelves a more organized and colorful look. Okay, maybe it is a bit OCD, but I liked it.

Anyway, my point is that while my bookshelves were not the exact arrangement I saw in the magazine, they did turn out to be a copy and shadow of what I saw. Today, we continue our look at the Old Testament tabernacle and study the most sacred Holy of Holies. Even in this room, the earthly dwelling of the presence of God, we find only a copy and shadow of a heavenly reality.

Let's read about this holy room from two difference places. First, let's go to Exodus.

Turn to **Exodus 25:10-40** and read this passage, noting every detail you find about the Holy of Holies, also called the Holy Place, and its contents.

_____

_____

_____

_____

_____

Now turn to **Hebrews 9:1-5** and note any additional detail you find in these verses, that was not included in the Exodus passage, about the Holy of Holies and the Ark.

_____

_____

_____

_____

You have just read about the earthly throne room of God. Do not gloss over this reading. Please don't allow familiarity to rob you of the enormity of what you just read. This is the place where God's presence dwelt on earth in the days of Moses. Unlike our churches today, this room was never entered by common people, nor was God easily accessible even to the priests. Only the high priest was allowed into the Holy of Holies, and then only once per year. In fear and trembling, and always with blood, he entered this room where the presence of God dwelt.

Think about the most sacred place you have ever visited. Where was it? What did you feel when you entered? Describe that here.

_____

_____

_____

_____

_____

_____

The focal point of this room—in fact, the only piece of furniture in the room—was the **Ark of the Covenant**. It was sometimes called the **Ark of the Testimony**, or simply the **Ark**. It, like many of the other pieces of furniture in the tabernacle, was fashioned of wood overlaid with gold, pointing forward to the humanity and divinity of the coming Christ. The mercy seat, also known as the atonement cover, was fashioned of pure gold and covered the top of the ark. It was on the atonement cover that the sacrifice for the sin of the people was offered by the high priest once each year on the Day of Atonement. Two cherubim, or angels, were fashioned out of gold as part of the atonement cover. Their wings were spread outward and upward over the cover, while their faces were turned in and down toward the mercy seat. The tablets upon which God wrote the Ten Commandments were placed inside the ark—commandments that were broken over and over by the people.

The significance of the ark and the mercy seat cannot be understated. It was the place where Holy God condescended to meet with sinful man. The ark was where God's mercy met man's sinfulness. This was the most sacred place in the world at that time. No singing took place; no preaching was heard; no money was given as an offering. Nothing that we consider to be part of "church" occurred in the Holy of Holies. The sole purpose of this place was for God to meet with man in the presence of a sacrifice offered to atone for man's sin. That's it. That was enough.

You and I have little frame of reference for the holiness of this room and the ark. Do you remember as a child going into a store with lots of beautiful china and crystal and your mother hissed at you, "Do NOT touch anything, or I will wear you out!" Well, this was that kind of place, only the consequences for misbehavior were much more severe than a spanking.

Let's take a trip back in time to King David's day in order to gain some perspective on the importance of the Ark of the Covenant. In the chapters leading up to 2 Samuel 6, David had been crowned and enthroned as King over Israel. The Philistine nation, Israel's archenemy, had been defeated and the people were celebrating. King David remembered that the Ark of the Covenant, which was central to worship in the Jewish religion, had neither been in the tabernacle, nor had it been brought into Jerusalem. Rather, it had resided in the house of Abinadab since the days of King Saul. David decided that it was time for the ark of God to reside in the temple in Jerusalem, so he and the people set out to get it.

Sounds like a worthy and good thing to do, right? What David forgot was that if you do the right thing in the wrong way, it is still wrong.

Turn back to the description of the crafting of the Ark of the Covenant in **Exodus 25:12-14**. What is being described in these verses?

_____

_____

_____

_____

Now, turn to **Numbers 4** where we find the duties of the sons of Kohath being described. The sons of Kohath were Levites, which means they were priests in the Old Testament tabernacle. The Kohathites were to be carriers of the furnishings in the tabernacle when the tabernacle moved according to God's direction. Note: Aaron and his sons were not Kohathites.

Fill in the blanks from the following verses:

- **Verse 15**: *After Aaron and his sons have finished covering the _____ _____ and all the holy articles, and when the camp is ready to move, the Kohathites are to come to do the _____. But they must not _____ the holy things or they will _____.*

- **Verse 20 (NIV1984)**: *But the Kohathites must not go in to_____ at the holy things, even for a _____, or they will _____.*

The poles that were placed in the rings in Exodus 25 were to be used to carry the ark any time it was moved.

Please turn now to **2 Samuel 6:1-7** and answer the following questions.

What task were David and his men setting out to accomplish? (verses 1-2)

_____

_____

What mode of transportation was used to move the ark to Jerusalem? (verse 3)

_____

_____

What were the names of the two men who were chosen to escort, or guide, the cart on which the ark rested? (verse 3)

_____

_____

What was taking place while the ark was being transported? (verse 5)

_____

_____

What happened in verse 6?

_____

_____

Verse 7 tells us the consequence of Uzzah's action from verse 6. What happened?

_____

_____

God had given explicit instructions to Moses and the Levites that the ark was to be carried by the poles on the shoulders of the Kohathites. Did David forget the instructions? Did the priests forget the instructions? Did David assume that because he was doing something "good" for God, he would be exempt from obeying God to the letter? Only in heaven will we know the answer, but you can bet your bottom dollar David had huge regrets about not following God's plan precisely. Someone wisely said, "Partial obedience is still disobedience," and David's attempt at bringing the ark to Jerusalem is a prime example of this truth.

Three months later, David attempted once again to bring the ark to Jerusalem, and this time he followed God's orders to the letter. The move came off without a hitch or a death. (2 Samuel 6:12-15) The Ark of the Covenant was the very throne of God on earth, and no one was allowed to touch it because of its holiness. God is serious about obedience to His Word. Even when it seems to be a small thing, like how a piece of furniture should be moved, God expects total obedience.

MEDITATION MOMENT:

Is there something God has asked you to do? Is there a change you need to make in your life in order to be in God's will? Has God spoken to your heart and said, "I want this"? Are you being obedient to do what He has asked, or are you following your own desires? Partial obedience is still disobedience. Delayed obedience is still disobedience. Spend some time talking with the Lord right now about this issue.

Day 4 – Hebrews 9 – The Better Tabernacle

I love to read. Recently, I have been reading some biographies and autobiographies of famous people. Currently, my reading is taking me into the biography of Steve Jobs, co-founder of Apple® Computers. Jobs was quite a character, and not always in a nice or amusing way; however, he was the driving force behind the wildly successful Apple® line of computers, tablets, and phones. In the early days of developing the Apple® I, Apple® II, Lisa, and Macintosh® computers, Jobs and his partner, Steve Wozniak, worked diligently to design machines that would be innovative and useful to the average consumer.

With each new computer, the pair built a prototype—an original computer from which all the others in the line would be mass-produced. The prototype computer was used by Jobs and Wozniak to demonstrate to prospective buyers the innovations developed by their team and used in each model. It was crucial to their work and marketing of the newest Apple® line.

This idea of building a prototype is not exclusive to the computer industry. Automobile manufacturers produce mind-blowing prototype cars to show off to the public. So do clothing manufacturers and many other industries. So did God. The Old Testament tabernacle, the focus of our last three days of study, was built from a prototype—an original from which the earthly tabernacle was modeled. In the Greek, the word *protos* lends the idea of being the first or the former. Let's take a look at the prototype, or the first tabernacle. There are three passages of Scripture from Hebrews we will study today.

Read the following passages and note every piece of information given about the prototype tabernacle.

Hebrews 8:1-5

_____

_____

_____

Hebrews 9:11

_____

_____

_____

Hebrews 9:23-24

_____

_____

_____

Let's consider several things from these verses—the first is that **the prototype tabernacle was set up in heaven by God**. Let me take you on a short journey through God's Word in order to help you see this.

In **2 Chronicles 30:27** the dwelling place of God is mentioned. Where is the dwelling place of God located?

_____

_____

God apparently wanted two homes, much like many people have a summer home and a winter home. Where does **Exodus 25:8-9** say God's "other" home (the home NOT in heaven) would be?

_____

_____

God dwelt in heaven until such time as He instructed Moses to build an earthly sanctuary where He would then dwell among His people, Israel. This does not mean God ceased existing in heaven, but rather that He was present on earth, as well as in heaven.

God's temple in heaven is mentioned again in **Revelation 11:19.** What familiar item do we find in the heavenly dwelling?

_____

_____

It seems the Ark of the Covenant gets around, doesn't it? We know from our study earlier this week that the Ark of the Covenant was placed in the Holy of Holies in the tabernacle in the wilderness. Yet, here it is in God's temple in heaven. Voila! The earthly tabernacle and furnishings were patterned after the heavenly tabernacle and furnishings.

Another important point about the heavenly tabernacle is that **it was purified with better sacrifices, the ultimate sacrifice of Jesus.** We'll discuss this study more next week when we read about those BETTER sacrifices.

The final thing I want you to see about the heavenly tabernacle is that **there was a place to sit within the prototype tabernacle.** Recall with me our discussion about a scarcity of chairs in the earthly tabernacle. There were a couple of altars, a candlestick, a table for bread, a basin to wash in, and the Ark of the Covenant….but NO chairs. Was God missing the gift of hospitality?

I love to entertain people. I love having them in for meals or just to sit and chat over a piece of dessert and coffee. *BUT*, I want them to go home when bedtime comes. I do not like having overnight company. I suppose it is some sort of a weird genetic defect within my DNA. When I know I am having overnight company, I stress out to the MAX. I don't know why I do it. Is it because I go to bed early, and I don't want to be forced to stay up late? Perhaps it is because I get up so early and want to go about my normal routine without having to worry about another person. Probably it is just because I am strange. I don't know. I just know that it really takes me out of my comfort zone to have overnight company. And to make it even weirder, I don't really like to spend the night at other people's homes. I'd much rather stay in a motel. Craziness!

Oh my, there I've gone and confessed my ultimate weirdness. I hope you still like me. I just hope you don't come to stay with me for an extended period of time!

Anyway, was God being a poor host by not placing chairs in the tabernacle on earth? No. He was symbolizing that the work of the priest was never completed. They had to constantly—day-after-day, week-after-week, month-after-month, year-after-year—minister in the tabernacle.

The heavenly tabernacle, on the other hand, apparently has seats.

What seat is referenced in **Isaiah 66:1**?

_____

_____

Fill in the blanks from **Mark 16:19 (NIV1984)**: *After the Lord _____ had spoken to them, he was taken up into _____ and he _____ at the _____ _____ of God.*

Because Jesus made the ultimate sacrifice, as we will learn next week, and because Jesus was the Better Priest, His work was finished once He died on the cross. When He ascended to heaven, He could take His seat beside God and focus on interceding for you and me. The heavenly tabernacle is a place of finished work and completeness. There is nothing more that needs to be done to secure eternal life for you and me.

MEDITATION MOMENT:

What is it about this marvelous heavenly tabernacle that speaks to your heart? Journal about it here.

Day 5 – All Access

Most of us have attended events where the event staff wore nametags that were coded in some way so as to indicate the degree of access the person had to the inner workings of the event, as well as to the star of the show. Some have access only to the audience area. Others have access to the box office or financial portions of the event, while still others are involved in the food service activities. Eventually, if you hang around long enough, you will find a very small group of people who have complete access to every part and person involved in the event. Each person in this group is close to the main attraction of the event and, perhaps, has a badge or nametag that says something like "ALL ACCESS."

Although nametags or badges were not used, the priests who served in the Old Testament tabernacle followed a similar procedure. In week 2, we learned about this. Let's review so we can have a proper perspective.

In Leviticus 1—7 we find details on the various offerings that were to be given to God on behalf of the Israelites. If we look closely, we will find that these offerings were to be offered by "the priests," who were Aaron and his sons in those first days of the tabernacle. (See Leviticus 1: 5; 2:2; 3:2). These sacrifices and offerings were to be performed at the altar of sacrifice, also known as the bronze altar. Because of the sheer number of sacrifices that were made, every anointed priest available was needed to perform these duties. In addition, the priests maintained the outer court of the tabernacle, which also included the bronze laver, or washbasin.

As you move into the tabernacle structure, you enter the Holy Place that contained the lampstand, the table of showbread, and golden altar of incense.

Turn to **Leviticus 24:1-8.** Who was to maintain the candlestick and table of showbread?

_____

_____

Now, please turn to **Exodus 30:7-10** and read about the person who would maintain the golden altar. Who was it?

_____

_____

In these verses we find that only Aaron, initially, or whoever occupied the office of high priest, had the responsibility for maintaining the Holy Place. While the "regular" priests had limited access to the tabernacle, the high priest had ALL ACCESS to the outer court and the Holy Place on a daily basis.

Now, let's move further into the tabernacle and check out the access to the Holy of Holies. There are several verses scattered throughout Leviticus 16 I would like for you to read.

In **Leviticus 16:2**, what warning was Moses to give Aaron, the high priest?

_____

_____

Why was it important for Aaron to heed this warning according the last part of **Leviticus 16:2**?

_____

_____

How did God describe the location of the Most Holy Place or Holy of Holies in **Leviticus 16:2**?

_____

_____

According to **Leviticus 16:11-12**, when Aaron went into the Most Holy Place or Holy of Holies, what three things was he to take with him?

_____

_____

Could the daily work of the tabernacle (i.e. the maintaining of the table, candlestick, and altar of incense) continue while Aaron was in the Holy of Holies? See **Leviticus 16:17** for the answer.

_____

_____

How often, according to **Leviticus 16:34,** was Aaron to enter the Most Holy Place or Holy of Holies?

_____

_____

_____

According to this same verse, what was the purpose of Aaron going into the Holy of Holies?

_____

_____

_____

While Aaron had an ALL ACCESS badge because of his position as high priest, he could not enter the Holy of Holies where the presence of God dwelt just any old time he felt like it. He could only enter once each year and then only in a carefully proscribed manner. It had to be, according to **Leviticus 16:34,** "as the Lord commanded Moses" in order to maintain the holiness of the place, as well as to remind the Israelites of Who God was.

Now, let's move to Hebrews and untie the bow and open this beautiful package straight from the heart of God. Turn with me to **Hebrews 10:19-23** and carefully read these verses.

When the high priest went through the veil in the tabernacle and into the presence of God, He did so in humility, fear, and trembling. I like the way the *New Living Translation (NLT)* words verses 19 and 20. Consider it.

19 And so, dear brothers and sisters, we can boldly enter heaven's Most Holy Place because of the blood of Jesus. 20 By his death, Jesus opened a new and life-giving way through the curtain into the Most Holy Place.

Circle the word in verse 19 that describes how you and I, as believers in Jesus Christ, can enter heaven's Holy of Holies, the very throne room of God.

_____

_____

In verse 20 what made it possible for you and me to boldly enter heaven's Most Holy Place?

_____

_____

_____

The way into the Old Testament tabernacle's Most Holy Place was shrouded, or hidden, by the veil or curtain. Turn to **Luke 23** where you will find the story of the crucifixion of Jesus. Fill in the blanks of **verses 44-46 (NIV1984)**.

It was now about the sixth hour, and darkness came over the whole land until the ninth hour, for the sun stopped shining. And the _____ of the _____ was _____ in _____. Jesus called out with a loud voice, "Father, into your hands I commit my spirit." When he had said this, he _____ his last (NIV1984).

Now, turn to **Mark 15:38**. What additional information are we given about this event?

_____

_____

At the very moment of Jesus' death on the cross, the veil of the temple that had kept people from the presence of God was split in two from top to bottom. ***From top to bottom***—not from bottom to top. Why is this so important? God made sure Mark told us the precise direction of the split in the curtain, so we would know that God Himself made a way for you and me to come into His presence…to come into His presence BOLDLY. The split in the curtain from top to bottom assured onlookers that the split was not made by man, but rather, by God. It was God's way of issuing a "come on in" invitation to anyone who was willing to enter through the blood of Jesus.

The God of all creation who laid the earth's foundation (Job 38:4), the One who hung the stars in the sky and holds the very world in the palm of His hand; God who gives orders to the morning and shows the dawn its place (Job 38:12), Yahweh, who knows where lightning originates (Job 38:24) and commands the eagle to soar (Job 39:27) welcomes you into His presence. This God, who dwells in unapproachable light, has opened the door of heaven's throne room and motioned for us to "come in my child and visit with Me."

But, I fear we take this for granted. Every person who has accepted Jesus' death on the cross as payment for her or his sin has had the door into the presence of God opened. Most of us will never sit and chat with the President of the United States or the Queen of England, but everyone who calls on the name of Christ has the opportunity to talk to God on a daily, even hourly, basis. **Boldly** we can come before Him. **Boldly** we can speak with Him. **Boldly** we can pour out our heart before Him. And we can do this with the assurance that He will not turn away. No matter what we have done or what shape we are in when we walk into His presence, He loves us and desires to be with us.

To think that a perfect, holy God would not only allow me to come BOLDLY into His presence, but would desire my company? I am undone over it. Completely undone! I am so unworthy because of my past, yet because of what Jesus did in the past, I am made worthy by His blood. HALLELUJAH!

Where are you today? Have you come boldly into the presence of God? Have you felt His arms of love wrap around you? Have you heard Him whisper to you, "I love you. I'm here for you. I will never leave you, no matter what." If you have not come boldly into His presence today, I invite you to do that. Please, no excuses that you are not ready or you are not good enough or you are not dressed up. He doesn't care! He just wants *you*! Go ahead. Knock on the door, push the door back, and BOLDLY walk forward into the waiting arms of your loving heavenly Father.

MEDITATION MOMENT:

Choose one of the Psalms listed here. Read it and respond to God out of it in prayer, in journaling, in singing, or in simply being quiet before Him. **Psalm 3; Psalm 16; Psalm 30; Psalm 34; Psalm 63: 1-8; Psalm 91**

WEEK FIVE

May I Serve You?

This week's recipe is one that has prompted smiles from literally hundreds of folks. Every year my mother makes dozens of loaves of pumpkin bread and gives them away. At any point in time, you will find at least 5-6 loaves in her freezer, just waiting to be bestowed on blessed friends.

I consider pumpkin bread to be a healthy dessert. Never mind the fact that it has mounds of sugar, eggs, and oil. It has pumpkin, and that is a healthy food as far as I'm concerned. So spread a tad of butter on it and enjoy it without the guilt, if possible!

The aromatic spices in this dessert call for a brew that goes down easy, such as Twinings® of London English Breakfast Tea or Eight O'Clock® Original Coffee.

RECIPE

Mom's Pumpkin Bread

3 cups sugar

1 cup oil

1 can (approx. 15 oz.) pumpkin

4 eggs

3 ½ cups cake flour

2 teaspoons baking soda

1 teaspoon baking powder

1 teaspoon salt

2/3 cup water

1 teaspoon each cinnamon, allspice, and nutmeg

½ teaspoon ground cloves

Mix ingredients in order, in mixing bowl with electric mixer. Beat well. Pour into 2 greased and floured loaf pans. Bake at 350 degrees for 1 hour and 15 minutes. Turn out of pan onto wire rack to cool.

NOTE: Best when made ahead and frozen. The moistness is increased and the flavor is enhanced by freezing.

Week 5 — A Better Sacrifice — The One Time for All Blend

I'm going to go ahead and warn you. This week of our study will not be for the faint of heart or the squeamish. The topic of sacrifice means that, inevitably, blood will be involved. There just isn't any way around it.

Speaking of blood, I'm reminded of the time, early in my first post-college job, when I learned to draw blood, or perform venipuncture. Drawing blood was the job of the nurses in the office, but I had a large volume of patients, and waiting on the nurses to finish with their patients and draw blood on my patients, ended up putting everyone behind in their work schedule. So, the decision was made that I should learn to perform blood draws on my own patients.

Cool! I wasn't squeamish and didn't think it would be a big deal until I was informed that I would do my first live venipuncture on my friend Joan. Eck! Not on my friend—on a stranger, maybe, but not on my friend.

Joan looked at me and assured me it was fine. It wasn't the first time she had been used as a guinea pig. So, I gathered up the needles, vacutainer, tubes, tourniquet, gauze, and alcohol pads and sat down beside Joan. And I sat, and I sat, and I sat. I knew what I had to do, but the actual doing of it on my friend seemed to be more than I could force myself to do.

Eventually, I gathered my courage and performed my first "stick." It went very well, and I went on to "stick" hundreds of people, from 4-year-olds to 80- year-olds, over the course of my research career. In fact, I became so proficient that many people *requested* that I do their venipuncture. I never drew blood, however, that I didn't think of the first time when I had to put the needle into my friend's arm.

I cannot imagine the feelings and thoughts going through the minds of the Israelites who had to slaughter an innocent lamb to cover their own sin. Perhaps you are not an animal person, but I am. While it was a lamb *and not a person*, it still had to be incredibly difficult to slit the throat of a beautiful, perfect lamb and watch the lifeblood drain from its veins.

Oh, but wait! That perfect innocent Lamb…it was a person! It was Jesus, the Son of God.

Join me as we "see" the perfect New Testament sacrifice in view of the imperfect sacrifice of the Old Testament.

Day 1 – Blood – The Gift of Life

Sacrifice. The word itself conjures up feelings of self-denial and maybe even self-ishness if we are really honest with ourselves. Most of us who live in America do not sacrifice very much. I heard a pastor talking about giving once. The question he asked penetrated my heart and convicted me to the core. He said, "How often do you give until it hurts?"

Sadly, my answer was "very rarely," especially when it comes to money. I give my time and my talent until I am stretched thin sometimes. That qualifies. But when it comes to my money, I don't give until it hurts nearly often enough.

Mind you, I'm not advocating giving money that you don't have and putting yourself in a financial bind. That would not be good stewardship. Instead, I am talking about giving money that you do have, but would rather use for lunch out with your girlfriends or a vacation or new outfit. Giving until it hurts requires sacrificing something else. It obligates us to say, "I can do this, but I know God wants me to do that."

Consider the definition of *sacrifice*.

Sacrifice – to give up (or the giving up) of something or somebody valued. [28]

With that definition in mind, let's do a bit of self-assessment here. This question is purely for personal use to help you decide where you fall on the scale of sacrificial living.

When was the last time you gave up/sacrificed something that you valued?

_____

_____

What did it cost you to make that sacrifice?

_____

_____

What is the greatest sacrifice you have ever had to make? What did it cost you to make that sacrifice?

_____

_____

I fear many of us cannot come up with anything significant we have had to sacrifice for the sake of another, or even for our own good. We are "I want it, and I want it right now, and I want it to be easy" kind of people. I am an "I want it, and I want it right now, and I want it to be easy" kind of girl. There you go. I just admitted to you that I do not sacrifice well. What about you?

As we begin to study the *better sacrifice* made by Jesus, I am going to ask you to read a significant portion of Scripture in the book of Hebrews and focus on only a few words. I think it is important that we gain context for the topic of sacrifice, and this seems to be the way the Holy Spirit is leading me to do it.

If you have access to colored pencils or two different colors of pens, please round them up. If possible, make sure one of them is red. You will see why in a moment.

Below I have provided you with a passage from Hebrews 9 and 10. Please read the entire passage and circle or mark in some way the following words:

- *Blood – use a red pen or pencil if possible*

- *Sacrifice(s)*

Once you complete your marking, answer the questions that follow the Scripture passages.

Hebrews 9:11-28

11 *But when Christ came as high priest of the good things that are now already here, he went through the greater and more perfect tabernacle that is not made with human hands, that is to say, is not a part of this creation.* **12** *He did not enter by means of the blood of goats and calves; but he entered the Most Holy Place once for all by his own blood, thus obtaining eternal redemption.* **13** *The blood of goats and bulls and the ashes of a heifer sprinkled on those who are ceremonially unclean sanctify them so that they are outwardly clean.* **14** *How much more, then, will the blood of Christ, who through the eternal Spirit offered himself unblemished to God, cleanse our consciences from acts that lead to death, so that we may serve the living God!*

15 *For this reason Christ is the mediator of a new covenant, that those who are called may receive the promised eternal inheritance—now that he has died as a ransom to set them free from the sin committed under the first covenant.*

16 *In the case of a will, it is necessary to prove the death of the one who made it,* **17** *because a will is in force only when somebody has died; it never takes effect while the one who made it is living.* **18** *This is why even the first covenant was not put into effect without blood.* **19** *When Moses had proclaimed every command of the law* to all the people, he took the blood of calves, together with water, scarlet wool and branches of hyssop, and sprinkled the scroll and all the people. *20* He said, "This is the blood of the covenant, which God has commanded you to keep." *21* In the same way, he sprinkled with the blood both the tabernacle and everything used in its ceremonies. *22* In fact, the law requires that nearly everything be cleansed with blood, and without the shedding of blood there is no forgiveness.

23 It was necessary, then, for the copies of the heavenly things to be purified with these sacrifices, but the heavenly things themselves with better sacrifices than these. *24* For Christ did not enter a sanctuary made with human hands that was only a copy of the true one; he entered heaven itself, now to appear for us in God's presence. *25* Nor did he enter heaven to offer himself again and again, the way the high priest enters the Most Holy Place every year with blood that is not his own. *26* Otherwise Christ would have had to suffer many times since the creation of the world. But he has appeared once for all at the culmination of the ages to do away with sin by the sacrifice of himself. *27* Just as people are destined to die once, and after that to face judgment, *28* so Christ was sacrificed once to take away the sin of many; and he will appear a second time, not to bear sin, but to bring salvation to those who are waiting for him.

Hebrews 10:1-18 (NIV1984)

1 The law is only a shadow of the good things that are coming—not the realities themselves. For this reason it can never, by the same sacrifices repeated endlessly year after year, make perfect those who draw near to worship. *2* Otherwise, would they not have stopped being offered? For the worshipers would have been cleansed once for all, and would no longer have felt guilty for their sin. *3* But those sacrifices are an annual reminder of sin. *4* It is impossible for the blood of bulls and goats to take away sin.

5 Therefore, when Christ came into the world, he said: *6* "Sacrifice and offering you did not desire, but a body you prepared for me; with burnt offerings and sin offerings you were not pleased.

7 Then I said, 'Here I am—it is written about me in the scroll—I have come to do your will, my God.'"

8 First he said, "Sacrifices and offerings, burnt offerings and sin offerings you did not desire, nor were you pleased with them"—though they were offered in accordance with the law. *9* Then he said, "Here I am, I have come to do your will." He sets aside the first to establish the second. *10* And by that will, we have been made holy through the sacrifice of the body of Jesus Christ once for all.

11 Day after day every priest stands and performs his religious duties; again and again he offers the same sacrifices, which can never take away sin. 12 But when this priest had offered for all time one sacrifice for sin, he sat down at the right hand of God, 13 and since that time he waits for his enemies to be made his footstool. 14 For by one sacrifice he has made perfect forever those who are being made holy. 15 The Holy Spirit also testifies to us about this. First he says: 16 "This is the covenant I will make with them after that time," says the Lord. "I will put my laws in their hearts, and I will write them on their minds." 17 Then he adds: "Their sin and lawless acts I will remember no more." 18 And where these have been forgiven, sacrifice for sin is no longer necessary.

Hebrews 9:11-14 talks about the blood of animals versus the blood of Jesus Christ. Note here what you learned about each.

_____

_____

_____

_____

_____

Hebrews 9:22 says that in order to provide forgiveness something must happen. What must happen?

_____

_____

_____

_____

Read **Hebrews 9:25-28** and **Hebrews 10:12-14** and note what Jesus sacrificed? How many times did He sacrifice? What did His sacrifice accomplish?

_____

_____

_____

_____

_____

_____

Great work today. You now have a solid base upon which to build the rest of our week of study about the _better sacrifice_. This is not the time to turn squeamish. We will be talking about blood often this week. Tomorrow we will take another look at the Old Covenant sacrifices. I know this study of Hebrews is deep and requires much of us, but our faith should be growing by leaps and bounds.

MEDITATION MOMENT:

At the beginning of today's lesson, I asked you about a sacrifice you had made. Now, I want you to consider a sacrifice another person (other than Jesus) made on your behalf. Perhaps it was your mom, who gave up her career to be a stay-at-home mom. Maybe it was your dad, who sacrificed resting in order to play ball with you when you were a kid. It might have been a teacher, who volunteered her or his time to tutor you. Perhaps it is a husband or wife, who works an extra job so you can stay home with your children. Write about the sacrifice that someone else made on your behalf, and then thank God for that person.

_____

_____

_____

_____

_____

_____

_____

Day 2 – The Sacrifice of Old

Yesterday, you had the opportunity to identify blood as a key component of the sacrifice talked about in the book of Hebrews. Blood really was central to the sacrifice and an integral part of the forgiving of sin. Today, we will spend more time at the Old Testament tabernacle, and watch as the sacrifices are brought to the priest and offered on the altar.

Earlier in our study, we learned the Old Testament tabernacle was made up of three distinct parts. There was the outer court where the bronze altar and bronze laver were positioned. This was the place where ordinary people brought their offerings for the covering of their sin. As you went further into the tabernacle complex, you saw the Holy Place, where only the priest could go on a daily basis. Beyond the altar of incense, and behind the heavy curtain, or veil, was the Holy of Holies that housed the Ark of the Covenant and the very presence of God. The high priest was the only person allowed in, and then only once a year, to offer a sacrifice for the atonement of the nation of Israel.

To you and me, the entire complex sounds rather grand and glorious—enough gold to redefine the word BLING! QVC could have broadcast from that building for years and not sold all the gold inside.

For all the grandeur of the Old Testament tabernacle, it is important for us to consider another aspect of it. The sacrifices that were offered, which made it possible for fellowship to be restored between God and man, were of prime importance and are worthy of some of our study time.

Read the following Scripture passages and match them to the sacrifice or offering they are detailing.

A. **Exodus 29:38-39**   _____ Peace/fellowship offering

B. **Exodus 30:1, 7-8**   _____ Grain offering

C. **Leviticus 1:3-5**   _____ Daily offering

D. **Leviticus 2:1-2**   _____ Trespass/Guilt offering

E. **Leviticus 3:1-2**   _____ Incense offering

F. **Leviticus 4:1-3**   _____ Sin offering

G. **Leviticus 5:5-6**   _____ Burnt offering

Many, many sacrifices and offerings. The first three sacrifices or offerings were voluntary: the burnt offering, the grain offering, and the peace offering. The final two sacrifices were required of the Israelite people: the sin offering and the trespass offering.

Now, let's look a bit more in-depth at a few of these. Go back to **Exodus 29:38**. Here we find the specifications for the daily offerings. In the Hebrew, daily means daily, every day. So every morning a spotless lamb was offered on the bronze altar, and every evening a spotless lamb was offered in the very same place—every morning and every evening for years upon years. Two lambs each day, 365 days each year. By my calculation, that is 730 lambs every year that were slaughtered as a sacrifice to God by the priests. That's a lot of lamb! Think of the blood from 730 lambs. Whoever had janitorial duty had quite a job, didn't they?

I've got news for you. That is not the end of the story.

Let's now consider just the compulsory or required sacrifices. Turn to **Leviticus 4** and answer the following questions:

According to **verse 2**, the sin offering or sacrifice was applicable when _____ sin unintentionally and does what is forbidden in any of the Lord's commands.

Ok, let's have a show of hands. How many of you have sinned unintentionally….today? Yes, you see my hand waving in the air. What did unintentional, or unwitting sin look like for the Israelites? We are told in Leviticus 5. Not speaking up to testify regarding something the person saw, touching anything unclean like the bodies of unclean, wild animals or unclean creatures on the ground, and thoughtlessly taking an oath to do anything. These are only a few of the things that qualified as unintentional sin. The Israelites had hundreds of laws they were required to keep so it would have been very easy to sin unintentionally and bring the necessity of sacrifice upon oneself.

Back to **Leviticus 4:3-4, 35**

Verse 3 details what should be sacrificed on the altar for unintentional sin. What was it?

_____

_____

What was the procedure for offering this sacrifice according to **verse 4**?

_____

_____

_____

Did you get that? The person who committed the unintentional sin had to bring the bull, lay their hands on the bull's head, and kill the thing right on the spot. That person's sin had caused the bull to be sacrificed, and God said that person had to be the one to kill the sacrifice. Ugh! This is gory, isn't it?

Let's move on.

- If one of the common people sinned unintentionally, either a goat **(Leviticus 4:28)** or lamb **(Leviticus 4:32)** could be brought, but it had to be an animal without defect. With either of these offerings, **verse 35 (NIV1984)** says that _the priest made _____ for the person for the _____ _____ committed._

Now, let's try to get a handle on the number of animals that were sacrificed in one year in the nation of Israel in the day of the Old Testament tabernacle. I'm not great with math, so you help me with my numbers.

- _Number of lambs sacrificed for the daily offering in a year (see above):_

  _____

- _Number of Israelite men who came out of Egypt with Moses according to_ **Exodus 12:37**_:_ _____

- _Let's be extraordinarily generous and assume each man only sinned unintentionally once a month. That would mean each man would sacrifice 12 animals per year at the altar so 600,000 x 12 =_ _____.

- _If we double the number to include the women of Israel, we have how many animals sacrificed each year for unintentional sin?_ _____

Add the daily sacrifices to that number and you get 14,400,730 animals sacrificed each year for the sin of the people of Israel. Fourteen and a half million animals sacrificed each year is a very conservative number (year after year to atone for the sin of the people). I'm not sure my mind can even wrap around that number. It would have been a continual parade of animals and people headed to the tabernacle. And the blood? Oh my! The blood flowed freely out the front gate of the tabernacle—the blood of spotless animals that were sacrificed to cover the sin of the people. Over and over, the people had to bring animals because the blood of a spotless animal only atoned for sin up to that moment. By the time they returned home from the tabernacle, many of them had sinned again, necessitating yet another animal be sacrificed. (I might as well have just set up my camper at the tabernacle because I would need to offer daily sacrifices. As I said, I was being generous when I assumed one unintentional sin per month.)

Fast forward to Paul's day when the temple sacrifices were soon to end. In 70 AD the Romans destroyed the temple. It has never been rebuilt. Observant Jews of today long for the time when the temple will be rebuilt, and the sacrifices will resume. Can you even imagine?

What the Jewish people do not understand is that there is no longer a need for those sacrifices to be made because the perfect and permanent sacrifice has been offered. More about that tomorrow.

MEDITATION MOMENT:

What thoughts are rolling around in your mind and heart about the millions of animals sacrificed to atone for sin over and over? Journal about it here, then pray for the Jewish people to have the eyes and hearts to see that no further sacrifices are necessary.

_____

_____

_____

_____

_____

_____

_____

_____

_____

_____

_____

Day 3 – The Sacrifices of the High Priest

A few times over the past five years, I have had the honor of administering communion for groups of ladies to whom I have spoken. It is always a holy moment for me. I feel quite inadequate to do it.

I recall the first time I was asked to assist a Methodist pastor as she offered communion to her ladies. I had spoken at their ladies' conference, and she wanted to finish the day with communion. What she failed to tell me until moments prior to communion was that she wanted me to help her offer the elements to the ladies. Now, I have taken communion many times in my life, but I had never administered communion to another person. I was stunned.

Seeing my deer-in-the-headlights look, that sweet pastor took me aside and gently explained that all I needed to do was hold the cup of wine for the ladies to dip their bread into and say to each, "His blood that was shed for you." That was it. I told her I could do that, and we proceeded to observe communion. I do not lie to you when I say I was as nervous as a long-tailed cat in a room full of rocking chairs! This was the *Lord's Supper*, for heaven's sake. What if I messed it up? What if I said the wrong words? What if my heart was not clean before God? What if God did not like women doing such things?

I think I might have felt just a tad of what the high priest felt on the Day of Atonement when he entered the Holy of Holies to offer the sacrifice of atonement on the mercy seat once each year. Come with me as we slip past the veil into the Holy of Holies and watch the high priest perform the ritual that will provide atonement for the sin of the people.

Leviticus 16 details the instructions for the sacrifice offered by the high priest on the Day of Atonement. Please read all of **Leviticus 16**. Once you have read this chapter, please note, which verse within the chapter details the activity being described in each sentence below. I will do the first one to show you what I am looking for.

Aaron, the high priest, could not enter the Holy of Holies any time he wanted to. If he did he would die. **Verse 2**

The high priest had to wear certain clothes to present the offering of Atonement. Verse _____

The high priest had to make a sacrifice for his own sin and that of his household first, using the blood of a bull. Verse _____

Once the high priest entered the Holy of Holies with the burning coals and fragrant incense, he sprinkled the blood of the bull on the atonement cover/mercy seat. Verse _____

The high priest then had to take the blood of a goat, the sin offering for the people, into the Holy of Holies and sprinkle it on the atonement cover. Verse _____

In this manner, atonement was to be made once each year. Verse _____

As you can see from your reading, the sacrifice of atonement had to be performed in a very specific manner and only once each year to cover, or atone, for the sin of the nation of Israel.

Now, let's turn back to **Hebrews 9.** I would like for you to see the beauty of the Old Testament as fulfilled by Christ in the New Testament, or as St. Augustine said, "The new is in the old concealed, the old is by the new revealed."

I began writing and giving you a synopsis of what happens in Hebrews 9, but I want you to read it for yourself and note what you find taking place the following verses:

Verse 7:

_____

_____

_____

Verse 11:

_____

_____

_____

_____

Verse 12:

_____

_____

_____

_____

Verses 13 -14:

_____

_____

_____

_____

Verse 25:

_____

_____

_____

_____

Verse 28:

_____

_____

_____

Isn't that spectacular? Jesus, the spotless Lamb of God, offered Himself as the perfect sacrifice that would, once and for all, take away the sin of all mankind. Never again would one more lamb, goat, or ram have to be slaughtered to cover sin temporarily. Never again would the priest have to limit himself to approaching God only once a year to offer a blood sacrifice for himself and the people. Never again would the Holy of Holies, the very throne room of God, be off limits to common people. _Never!_ Jesus was the BETTER Priest who offered the BETTER sacrifice, His very life, to atone for my sin and yours. His death on the cross opened the way for us to visit with God anytime we desire and for our hearts to be made clean.

In his insightful commentary on the book of Hebrews entitled _Be Confident_, Warren Wiersbe relates a story of sharing a conference with a Christian psychiatrist whose teachings were biblically on target. The psychiatrist told Wiersbe that "the trouble with psychiatry is that it can only deal with symptoms. A psychiatrist can remove a patient's _feelings_ of guilt, but he cannot remove the guilt. It's like a trucker loosening a fender on his truck so he won't hear the motor knock. A patient can end up feeling better, but have two problems instead of one." [29]

The sacrifice of Christ did something that the Old Testament sacrifices could never do. The Old Testament sacrifices symbolized the cleansing of sin, but could never cleanse the person's heart. Jesus' sacrifice accomplished the internal cleansing of the heart, and made it possible for all who would accept Him to become new creations.

According to **2 Corinthians 5:17,** what happens to anyone who is in Christ (accepts His sacrifice to cover their sin)?

_____

_____

_____

Read **Hebrews 10:11-14** and write it out in its entirety in the space below.

_____

_____

_____

_____

There is so much in that passage that nearly takes my breath away. When the book of Hebrews was written (approx. AD 67-69) the Temple was still standing, and the priests were still offering sacrifices. Why? Because the Jewish people did not understand that the ultimate Sacrifice had been made by Jesus Christ. I can almost imagine Jesus, seated beside the Father in heaven, the BETTER tabernacle, shaking His head and saying, "If only they understood. It is finished."

MEDITATION MOMENT:

It is finished, my friend. There is no need for sacrifices or works to make you right with God. Jesus did the work. Jesus has already done everything that is needed. Consider whether you are still relying on any kind of good works or deeds to make you acceptable to God. Will you lay down those works and deeds at His feet and allow His sacrifice to cover your sin? Even if you already know Jesus as Lord and Savior, you may still be trying to work your way into God's favor. You don't have to—the work was done on the cross by Jesus. Have you accepted that it truly is finished?

Day 4 – What Pleases God?

If I asked a dozen people what the best feeling in the world is, I would likely get a dozen different answers. Feelings are incredibly subjective. They depend on circumstances, physical health, emotional stability, and so much more. Here are some possible answers to my question:

- *To be in love and know that you are loved back*

- *Becoming a mommy or a daddy*

- *Getting a job promotion*

- *Having a book published*

- *Speaking to large groups*

- *Helping someone who is in trouble*

- *Going on vacation just to rest…and actually resting*

- *Taking your son on his first hunting trip*

- *Spending time with friends*

All of these are wonderful things and offer a sense of well-being, but there is something else that I have found to be the absolutely best, most wonderful feeling in all the world. Author Max Lucado wrote an entire book about this feeling, and he called it *Cure for the Common Life: Living in Your Sweet Spot*. For those of you who don't know about a "sweet spot," allow me to elaborate. The sweet spot on a tennis racquet or baseball bat is that small area where the mechanics of hitting a ball work optimally. It is the area that, when the ball hits it, produces the most power and accuracy, and the least amount of error.

Trust me, we are not going to talk about tennis or baseball. I don't like baseball, and I'm a lower than average tennis player. In fact, when I played tennis, I found the sweet spot on the tennis racquet far fewer times than I would have liked. No, today we will talk about living in the sweet spot of life. The most wonderful feeling in the world is living in the center of God's will—that place where you know you are doing and being exactly what God desires at that specific moment of your life. Really, this is a better feeling than feasting on a plate of chicken and dumplings, followed by a big slice of chocolate cake, accompanied by a glass of cold milk.

Jesus knew about living in His sweet spot. Join me as we begin our day in **Hebrews 10:5-7**.

What words or phrases in that passage speak to the issue of Jesus living in the sweet spot of God's will?

_____

_____

_____

Before we forge ahead, I want to point out that this passage in Hebrews is not an original to the author of the book. Any time you see a passage indented and/or with quotation marks around it, you can be pretty sure it came from somewhere else in the Bible. So it is with Hebrews 10:5-7. Although the wording is slightly different, the author of Hebrews pulled this passage from **Psalm 40:6-8**. Take a moment and read it from Psalm 40.

For the next few minutes let's think about living in the will of God. It is important for us to realize that living in the will of God is more than just _doing_ the things God asks or expects of us. It is very much about having a heart that desires to please God. Let's allow Jesus to be our example in finding our sweet spot in God's will.

We spent a week earlier in this study examining the Christology of Jesus—the fact that He was the Son of God who came to earth to die on the cross, to pay the price you and I owed for our rebellion against God.

From beginning to end, Jesus lived in the Father's will. Was it always easy? Not exactly. Sometimes it meant He caused His earthly parents great angst. Consider the time when He was 12 years old and was inadvertently left behind in Jerusalem while His family headed back home to Galilee. In truth, He was not left behind, although His parents felt He was. He purposely stayed behind.

Turn to **Luke 2:48-50** and note the reason Jesus gave His mother for staying behind in Jerusalem.

_____

_____

_____

Even as a young boy, Jesus knew the reason He was on earth and had a heart that was totally submitted to God's will.

How does **Luke 2:52** add to our understanding of Jesus living in the sweet spot of God's will?

_____

_____

The prophet Isaiah foretold the obedience of Christ to the will of God in Isaiah 11. In verses 1-3 he prophesied that the Messiah, Jesus Christ, would have the Spirit of the Lord upon Him, and His delight would be in the fear or respect for God.

Jesus talked about this idea of living in the sweet spot of God's will in John 6 and John 15, although He did not exactly use the words "sweet spot." Let's look at John 6 first.

Write out **John 6:38** in the space below and circle the words or phrases that hint at sweet spot living.

_____

_____

_____

_____

Please read **John 15:9-10** and write out the portion of these two verses that gives you more insight into Jesus' sweet spot living.

_____

_____

_____

I especially like the way _The Message Bible_ phrases the verses from John 15.

> _I've loved you the way my Father has loved me. Make yourselves at home in my love. If you keep my commands, you'll remain intimately at home in my love. That's what I've done—kept my Father's commands and made myself at home in his love._

Sweet spot living means that we are at home where we are most comfortable— most productive—and willingly doing what God wants us to do.

Please look back now at our focal passage for today from **Hebrews 10:5-8** and record what God said does not get us in the sweet spot of God's will.

_____

_____

_____

_____

More than anything—more than sacrifices, more than offerings, more than good deeds--more than anything, God desires a heart that is wholly committed to loving and following Him. When you and I love Jesus with our whole heart and are willing to live a life that reflects His life, we find ourselves living in our sweet spot…firmly situated in the will of God.

As we close today, let's look at one more verse in God's Word that speaks "sweet spot" so tenderly to me. **Isaiah 30:15 (NKJV)** says:

> _In returning and rest you shall be saved; In quietness and confidence shall be your strength._

It is only in turning to Jesus in quietness and confidence, knowing that He is in control and He will do what is best for us, that we can find our sweet spot in God's will. We must repent of sin, rest in the love and grace of our Lord, and trust our lives to His heart.

MEDITATION MOMENT:

Are you living in your sweet spot? Are you squarely in the middle of God's will for your life? If not, how long has it been? What would it take for you to get back to that place of sweet spot living? Take a moment to journal your thoughts here and then ask God to help you find, or return to, the "sweet spot" of His will for your life.

Day 5 - Draw Near

The word "panorama" is one that brings to mind wide-open views and vistas. I think of standing on the edge of a scenic overlook on the Blue Ridge Parkway in North Carolina and looking out over the beautiful mountains. No matter which way I turn I see mountains and trees and beauty.

I am also reminded of the time I stood on top of Mount Megiddo (Har-megiddo or Tell Megiddo) in the land of Israel and looked out over the Jezreel Valley. I could see lush and fertile fields in the valley below where cotton and other crops were being grown. These scenic overlooks provide a panoramic or comprehensive view of the beauty of God's creation.

While the panoramic views I described above provided incredible sights in a big-picture kind of way, I found it was impossible to pick out small details in each place because of the distance. Detail is sacrificed for scope in a panoramic view.

Today, we are going to have the opportunity to take a panoramic look at our entire Hebrews Bible study in the space of only a few wonderful verses in Hebrews chapter 10. We will be able to look at the entire scope of our study, but not the intricate details. These five verses from Hebrews 10 incorporate the BETTER priest, the BETTER tabernacle, the BETTER covenant and the BETTER sacrifice. Let's take a look at them.

Read **Hebrews 10:19-23** and note any words or phrases that speak of each of the elements of our study.

The **BETTER** Priest –

_____

_____

The **BETTER** Tabernacle –

_____

_____

The **BETTER** Covenant –

_____

_____

The **BETTER** Sacrifice –

_____

_____

These five verses hold such hope for those who are believers in Jesus Christ. I want us to treat them like a delicious piece of cake today; let's take them in slowly and savor each one in order to fully comprehend what the Lord is saying to us.

Write **Hebrews 10:19** here.

_____

_____

_____

_____

_____

_____

_____

I hope the translation of the Bible you have uses the word "confidence" in this verse, but if not, you might have the word "boldly." When I researched the meaning of the original Greek word used here, I got as excited as if you had offered me a double-blended Strawberry Frappuccino with extra whipped cream on top.

The Greek Word is _parresia_ and it means: "Freedom in speaking. Confidence or boldness, particularly in speaking." Especially in Hebrews and 1 John, the word denotes confidence, which is experienced with such things as faith in communion with God, in fulfilling the duties of an evangelist, holding fast our hope, and deeds, which imply a special exercise of faith. _Parresia_ is possible as the result of guilt being removed by the blood of Jesus Christ and manifests itself in confident praying and witnessing." [30]

This confidence the writer of Hebrews speaks of is one that is not gained because of anything you or I have done. Rather it is a confidence that is available to us because of what Jesus accomplished when He died on the cross. Because of His death, you and I now have a "come anytime invitation" into God's presence. We don't have to stand outside God's throne room in fear of entering His presence. We can boldly throw open the door of the throne room through prayer and be accepted into His presence anytime we desire it. He is our Daddy, our

Abba, and He is pleased when we desire to be with Him. So, do not fear being rejected, but rather go boldly and with confidence into His presence wearing your "ALL ACCESS" badge that was given to you by Jesus.

Write **Hebrews 10:20** here.

_____

_____

_____

_____

This verse is one that contains a word that seems to be self-explanatory, but when you dig into its meaning you find so much more. The word "new" in this verse has an incredible depth of meaning. The Greek word is *prosphatos,* and it means "newly or recently slain." This verse could read "by a newly slain, yet also Living Lamb." The writer is contrasting the Old Covenant sacrifice of a spotless lamb whose death covered the sin for the moment with the Spotless Lamb who died, lives again, and covers our sin for all time. But wait, He not only covers our sin; He washes our hearts and makes them new. Jesus is the Lamb that opened the way for you and me to boldly enter God's throne room.

Write **Hebrews 10:21** here.

_____

_____

_____

_____

Who is that "great high priest over the house of God"?

_____

What was the primary function of the high priest in the tabernacle? (Remember our study of the priesthood and the tabernacle.)

_____

_____

_____

_____

Since Jesus has gone into the Holy of Holies and offered that ultimate sacrifice…

Write **Hebrews 10:22** here.

_____

_____

_____

_____

Do you hear it? Do you hear the Father calling? "Come on in, Leah. Pull up a chair, sit a spell, tell Me what is going on in your world." Ah, but wait! You can only pull up a chair and sit a spell with God if you have first invited Jesus to be the payment for your sin and rebellion. For those who have not accepted Jesus as Lord and Savior, there is no "ALL ACCESS" badge that allows them into God's throne room. Has your heart been sprinkled with the blood of Jesus? Have you been washed clean?

Write **Hebrews 10:23** here.

_____

_____

_____

I can almost hear the conviction in the voice of the writer of Hebrews as he delivers this sermon. Hold on to the hope of seeing Jesus! Hold on to the hope of eternity where there will be no more sorrows or difficulties! Hold on to the hope that Jesus walks beside you to help you in this journey called life. Hold on! Don't give up! Don't give in! Don't give out! Why? Because the One who died for your sin promised He would make good on every promise, and He is faithful to keep His promises.

You cannot find one promise in the Word of God that God has not kept or will not keep. If God promises it, it is as good as done. Oh, we may not get to see the promise fulfilled in our lifetime; but never fear, God keeps His promises. So hold on to your hope and faith. Don't let the trials of life knock down your faith. Hold on to the One who holds you.

MEDITATION MOMENT:

Are there circumstances in your life that cause you to be discouraged in your faith? List them here. Once you have made your list, I invite you to pray the following over each item on your list:

_____

_____

_____

_____

_____

_____

_____

_____

_____

_____

_____

_____

"Dear God, help me to hold on to my hope and faith, even in the midst of (name your trial here) _____ .
I know that Jesus made a way for me to come into Your presence and stand before You. Right now I ask You to give me peace and wisdom concerning this trial. Show me what You desire for me to learn from it. Help me to be faithful to You because You are faithful to me."

May I Serve You?

We are pound cake people here at the Adams' house. We don't shun other desserts, but pound cakes are really what we like best. The Five Flavor Pound Cake is one of our favorites. In fact, at Christmas I bake about a dozen of these cakes to give as gifts. You should see how eyes light up when the cakes arrive at their intended destinations. The Five Flavor Pound Cake recipe has been around a while, and it is unique in that it is one of the moistest pound cakes I have ever eaten. It is almost inaccurate to call it a pound cake because most pound cakes are dense and firm. Not the Five Flavor Cake! It is soft, incredibly moist, and mouth-watering good. I predict this cake will become a favorite in your house, just like it is in mine.

Brew up a cup of Starbucks® Blonde Decaf and enjoy it with a piece of this cake after dinner.

RECIPE

FIVE FLAVOR POUND CAKE

2 sticks butter (no substitutions), softened

1/2 cup shortening (Crisco® or similar brand)

3 cups sugar

5 eggs

3 cups cake flour

1/2 teaspoon baking powder

1 cup milk

1 teaspoon each lemon, vanilla, coconut, rum, and butter flavorings

Preheat oven to 325 degrees F. Grease and flour a tube or Bundt pan. Cream together margarine, shortening, and sugar for 5-7 minutes, or until light and fluffy. Add eggs one at a time and beating no more than 20 seconds after each addition. Sift baking powder with cake flour and add alternately to batter with milk, mixing only enough to incorporate flour. Remove beaters from mixer and add flavorings. Stir by hand to incorporate flavorings. Pour into prepared pan. Bake 1 hour and 30 minutes. Cool in pan for 1 hour then turn out onto wire rack.

Glaze

1 cup sugar

1/2 cup water

1 teaspoon each above flavorings

Bring all glaze ingredients to a boil. Pour glaze over cake after turning cake out onto wire rack to cool.

Week 6 – A Better Faith: Café Faith

How in the world do you take one of the most familiar and beloved chapters in the entire Scriptures and make it speak in a fresh way to your audience?

I have no idea. *Just being honest here.*

It was my dilemma as I wrote this Bible study. The Hall of Faith. What could be said that hadn't already been said?

More than once, I told the Lord that this was all His idea, and it was His responsibility to show me how to deal with such an important chapter in Hebrews. More than once He said, "I know, and I will."

Guess what? He did.

This week will be different than the previous five weeks. While you have had an opportunity each day to do some heart work through our Meditation Moment sections, the final days of this week will require even more heart (and brain) work. In this study on faith, there has to be a time and place for you to consider your own faith journey. This is the week. I hope you enjoy it and come out on the other side more certain than ever of the solidity of your faith in Jesus Christ.

Day 1 – Remember and Endure

I have an affinity for great quotes and stories. In fact, I keep a file on my computer entitled "Quotes." It is chock full of quotes from all sorts of people. I use it a lot, especially when I am writing. I think the wisdom, and sometimes the lunacy, of other people is something God uses to instruct and encourage us. When I am preparing to write a message or post for my blog, part of my prayer preparation is to ask the Lord to show me any quotes or stories He desires for me to use to help illustrate His message.

Here are a few of my favorites:

"You can't make your candle burn brighter by blowing out someone else's candle." Author Unknown

"God is too good to be unkind; He is too wise to be mistaken. When you cannot trace His hand, you can always trust His heart." C.H. Spurgeon

"I have been driven many times upon my knees by the overwhelming conviction that I had nowhere else to go." Abraham Lincoln

"It is the image of God reflected in you that so enrages hell; it is this at which the demons hurl their mightiest weapons." William Gurnall

"Much of the beauty of obedience lies in its being rendered at once and without question." C.H. Spurgeon

"Intercessory prayer touches God with one hand while reaching out to those being prayed for with the other." Jim Cymbala

"He is no fool who gives what he cannot keep to gain what he cannot lose." [31] Jim Eliot

"We cannot measure the eternal significance of present faithfulness." [32] James Denison

"It's always too soon to give up on God." [33] James Denison

"God is the One who builds trophies from the scrap pile—who draws His clay from under the bridge—who makes clean instruments of beauty from the filthy failures of yesteryear." [34] Charles Swindoll

"When a train goes through a tunnel and it gets dark you don't throw away the ticket and jump off. You sit still and trust the engineer." Corrie ten Boom

"Faith is putting God in every fill-in-the-blank." [35] Beth Moore

As we begin this week of study on the topic of faith, let's return to Hebrews chapter 10 and harvest a basket full of encouragement from the writer to keep holding on to our faith, especially in the rough spots, because in the end we will be rewarded.

In today's focal passage, the writer uses quotes from the Old Testament to remind his audience of the importance of staying faithful. In addition, he throws in some mighty fine quotes of his own. Let's look at all of it. Please turn to **Hebrews 10** and read verses **26-39**.

Recall with me that the writer of Hebrews is likely speaking to a group of Jewish Christians who have been and are being persecuted for their faith in Christ. They are, at the very least, entertaining the notion of returning to the way of Judaism in an effort to avoid persecution.

In verses 26 – 29, the writer employs the use of that wonderful tactic used by parents around the world to encourage their children toward obedience. It is the old do-you-remember-what-happened-the-last-time technique. In this case, the writer uses **Deuteronomy 19:15** as a teaching tool.

According to Mosaic Law, how many witnesses were required to convict a person of rejecting the Law?

_____

The writer is attempting to drive home the gravity of turning away from the gospel. If it only took two or three witnesses to bring *death* upon a person who rejected the Mosaic Law, how much worse would the punishment be for someone who turned their back on Jesus and the blood He shed on Calvary?

The Law was God's instruction, but Jesus was God's Son. The visual of trampling or walking on the Son of God is one that would have been understood completely by the writer's audience. In that day, the feet were the filthiest part of the body. To walk on or trample something or someone indicated a total disregard for that person or thing. To reject the gospel and turn back to the ways of Judaism would be a monumental affront to God, and an epic failure because it was a rejection of His Son.

As the writer goes into the final verses of Hebrews 10, I can almost see him shaking his finger at the audience and telling them they had better be very careful how they act because God will not let disobedience slide by. Please re-read **Hebrews 10:30-31**.

Look up the references to the two quotes the writer uses in verse 30. They are found in **Deuteronomy 32:35-36, then continue reading through verse 42.**

How might this passage have been a wake up call to the audience of the writer of Hebrews?

_____

_____

_____

_____

_____

_____

_____

The writer of Hebrews then shifts the focus from the Israelites of Moses' day to the days in the recent past of his audience. He uses positive reinforcement to encourage them in their faith walks.

In Hebrews 10:32, the NKJV uses the words "stood your ground" to describe what the Jewish Christians had done in the face of suffering earlier in their lives. The Greek word for "stood your ground" is *hypomeno,* and it lends the idea of remaining, enduring, or persevering under stress. Apparently, these Jewish Christians had seen persecution and had been successful in remaining strong in their faith in the past.

Hebrews 10:33 goes on to detail some of what had gone on. List below what these Christians had faced.

_____

_____

_____

_____

In **verse 34**, what reason does the author give for the Christian leaders having successfully endured their earlier suffering?

_____

_____

_____

_____

_____

Perhaps you can identify? Different seasons in our lives bring different strengths and weaknesses. Although it has not happened often, I have battled mild depression a couple of times in my life. When I am in the midst of the dark shadows of depression, I am far less capable of handling stresses that would normally not even be a blip on my stress radar. It doesn't always have to be an emotional issue that causes us not to be able to handle stressful situations. It could be marital difficulties, employment issues, financial issues, or Lord have mercy, mood swings. The bottom line is that sometimes you and I just don't cope as well with stress as we do at other times.

For whatever reason, the Jewish Christians being addressed in Hebrews were not enduring their current season of persecution well. The pastor of the church, the author of Hebrews, took extra special care to encourage them to stand firm in their faith and not forsake the gospel because there would be great reward. He finished the chapter by reminding them of the ultimate reason for faithfulness.

What does **verse 36** say is the ultimate reward for remaining faithful to the gospel?

_____

_____

_____

Receiving the promise. What promise? The promise of forgiveness of sin. The promise of Christ living within them through the presence of the Holy Spirit. The promise of eternal life.

Turn to the book of Revelation. Read **Revelation 21:22—22:5**. Note below every benefit that will ultimately belong to those who remain faithful to Jesus Christ.

MEDITATION MOMENT:

Faithfulness to the gospel of Jesus Christ may cost us a little or it may cost us our very lives. When we measure the cost against the rewards that await us, it is worth it. Please choose one or two benefits from the list you just made and turn them into a prayer of praise to God for making eternal life available through the blood of Jesus Christ.

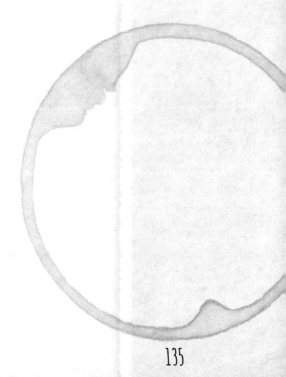

Day 2 – What Difference Does Faith Make?

My husband and I are similar in many ways. Over the years of being married, we have discovered many things about one another. Things like the fact that neither of us likes liver. To be honest with you, he would have been up the creek without a paddle if he had liked liver, because I am not sure I could have made myself cook the stuff! It is just nasty as far as I am concerned.

We both enjoy camping. We like good food. We both love Jesus. We are mountain people rather than beach bums. Both of us can get ridiculously excited about strawberry shortcake from The Cheesecake Factory®. We are united on the fact that there are few things that bless us more than a plate of my special collard greens, soup beans, and cornbread.

There are some differences between us, however. He likes Miracle Whip®. I'm a mayo girl. He's a hunter. I'm an indoor woman. He enjoys a good western. They bore me to tears. He understands football. I sometimes struggle to even find the ball on the field.

One major difference between us is how we react to a story. Greg wants the Webster's® Unabridged Version of most everything. I am the CliffsNotes® type. When I tell him about something that happened to someone, I give the basic information. Who, what, when, where, how, why. He will then ask me, "Well, what about this? Or what about that?" To which I usually respond, "I don't know. I'm telling you everything I know." He just wants more details than I have or am willing to take the time to remember. I just want the facts, ma'am. He wants the facts plus the backstory.

Are either of us wrong? No, we are just different.

As we come to **Hebrews 11**, I am excited because it is a classic CliffsNotes® chapter. It gives the basic facts about some of the giants of faith in the Bible. If you want more details, you can delve into them, but you don't have to in order to get the substance of the story.

Please read **Hebrews 11** and count the number (circle or underline them in your Bible, if you dare) of times the phrase "by faith" is used. How many did you find?

So, if you had to guess, what is the overarching theme of **Hebrews 11**?

_____

_____

If you said "living by faith" you are right. This chapter has been given several names such as God's Hall of Faith, The Saints Hall of Fame, The Honor Roll of Old Testament Saints, and others. This is the place where the author of Hebrews grew nostalgic and began to think back over the years and say, "By faith, look what so-and-so did. How I esteemed them!" It is almost like taking a walk through a museum of beautifully painted portraits of the life of the spiritual giants of the Old Testament. Imagine it. Standing in front of the beautiful oil painting of the life and faith walk of Abraham and "oohing" and "aahing" over his faithfulness… in spite of his mistakes. Remember, sometimes the errors in a masterpiece increase the value. So, it is with God's faithful ones.

It is impossible, in the space allotted in this week of study, to visit with each of the people mentioned in **Hebrews 11**. I wish we could, but then we might still be studying the eleventh chapter of Hebrews for years. Let's look at **Hebrews 11** in a unique way that allows us to enter into some of the stories of the people mentioned in this chapter.

I want us to peer into the lives of two of the Old Testament greats as if we were their contemporaries, living in their town, our kids playing with their kids, rubbing elbows with them at the city gate. Let's answer a key question: what difference did their faith in God make in their lives and the lives of those around them?

Today, begin by writing out **Hebrews 11:1** in the space below.

_____

_____

_____

_____

This will be our guidestone, our true north. As we look at these lives, we will return repeatedly to this definition of faith in order to answer our key question.

In *Be Confident,* Wiersbe said, "True Bible faith is confident obedience to God's Word in spite of circumstances and consequences." [36] Let's use this quote from Wiersbe and Hebrews 11:1 as we look today at the first man of faith, Abel, the son of Adam and Eve.

Summarize here what **Hebrews 11:4** says of Abel.

_____

_____

_____

_____

Let's go back to Genesis 3—4 to learn a bit about Abel and get the story behind the story.

Using **Genesis 3:8** as a reference, what can we assume about the relationship between God and His human creation prior to this verse?

_____

_____

If you said they had a face-to-face relationship, you would be right. In Genesis 3:8, Adam and Eve are hiding from God as He takes His walk in the garden in the cool of the day. Because they hid, I think it is safe to assume they knew God would be strolling through at about that time of day. I believe this had been a daily habit of the Almighty—a time when He communed with His creation.

What happened in **Genesis 3:23-24**?

_____

_____

Adam and Eve, because of their disobedience to God, were banished from the Garden of Eden and thus, from God's presence. Never again would they have a face-to-face relationship with their Creator.

Genesis 4:1 details a first. What was it?

_____

_____

_____

The first recorded birth—that of Cain, is found in Genesis 4:1. The birth of Abel follows in verse 2. These two boys were the first humans to not have a face-to-face relationship with God. They would have to walk out their earthly journeys by faith.

Now read **Genesis 4:1-15** and answer the following questions:

When Cain and Abel grew to manhood, they each chose jobs. List here what each did to make a living.

_____

What ritual do verses 3-4 tell us about?

_____

_____

What did Cain bring as an offering?

_____

_____

What did Abel bring as an offering?

_____

_____

What piece of information does the biblical text leave out of verses 4-5 that would help us understand why God accepted one offering and rejected the other?

_____

_____

Okay, that last question was not a trick question, but it might have been a bit difficult to understand; however, I wanted you to think it through. The Bible does not tell us anything about the instructions God gave to Cain and Abel prior to verse 3 concerning offerings. It seems like an important piece of information, but we must trust that God has divulged exactly what we need to know.

I read these verses over and over again and asked the Lord for clarity. As a result, I want to suggest one possible reason why Abel's offering was accepted and Cain's was not. Genesis 4:3 says that Cain brought "some of the fruits of the soil," while Abel brought "fat portions from some of the firstborn of his flock."

Even though Moses and the Israelites lived hundreds of years after Abel, how might **Exodus 34:19** shed light on the issue of Abel's acceptable offering?

_____

_____

Hundreds of years later, God would tell the Israelites that every firstborn belongs to Him…their firstborn child, their firstborn animals…every firstborn was dedicated to the Lord.

Colossians 1:15 may add another piece to the puzzle. What does it call Jesus, the BETTER Sacrifice?

_____

_____

_____

Could it have been that God had already made clear to Adam and his family that He expected the firstborn or first fruits to be offered to Him? I don't know for sure, but if that was the case and Cain only brought "some" of his fruits, rather than the first fruit of his labor, it would not have pleased God. In fact, it would have signaled that Cain, like his parents, was rebellious and eager to go his own way.

I'm partial to John MacArthur's thoughts on this topic:

> "There was nothing intrinsically wrong with a grain or fruit or vegetable offering. The Mosaic covenant included such offerings. But the blood offerings were always first, because only the blood offerings dealt with sin." [37]

> He goes on to say, "In Abel's sacrifice, the way of the cross was first prefigured. The first sacrifice was Abel's lamb—one lamb for one person. Later came the Passover—with one lamb for one family. Then came the Day of Atonement—with one lamb for one nation. Finally came Good Friday—one Lamb for the whole world." [38]

For all the unanswered questions we have about this story, we know that Abel offered his lamb by faith and God accepted it. What difference did faith make in Abel's life? It brought the smiling nod of God's approval. His faithful obedience earned him a place in God's Hall of Fame. Did it save him from violence? No. But Abel has the distinction of being the first martyr of the faith, and I imagine that will earn him a special crown in heaven to cast at the feet of Jesus.

How did Abel's faith impact those around him? Not everyone rises to the occasion, and Cain's true nature of rebellion and jealousy was brought out by Abel's obedient faith. Cain's punishment by God for killing Abel was a reminder to everyone for generations to come of the consequences of disobedience to God.

MEDITATION MOMENT:

Being obedient to God is not always easy, as Abel found out. Journal about a time when you experienced a difficult obedience, yet you were blessed because you walked in faith and did what God asked.

_____

_____

_____

_____

_____

_____

_____

_____

_____

_____

_____

_____

_____

_____

_____

_____

Day 3 – By Faith Sarah...

Behind every successful man there is a good woman, or so the saying goes. Not a perfect woman, but a good woman. Although the Hagar situation *was* an epic fail on Sarah's part, I'm voting for Sarah, aka Mrs. Abraham, as saint of the year if it comes up for a vote. Think about what the poor woman endured over the course of her life at the hands of Abraham.

Her life was fine and dandy until one day Abraham told her, "Saddle up, we are moving to a new place. Oh, and by the way, I don't really know where we are going…we are just going and will figure it out on the way." Eek!

Have mercy! No woman in her right mind would be thrilled about that. What about the house? What can I take with me? The silver? The china? My favorite chair? How many clothes can I take on those donkeys? Will there be a good doctor there? And where will I get my hair done in the new town?

As if that were not bad enough, Abe decided that she should say she was his *sister* when they rolled into the big city. You see, she was quite a looker, Sarah was, and Abraham was afraid the king would have him killed in order to make Sarah part of his harem if word got out they were married. Well, Abraham's plan nearly got Sarah married off to the king! Had it not been for the plagues the Lord brought on the king, Sarah would have been Mrs. Pharaoh rather than Mrs. Abraham.

Then there was the business with Lot. He was a selfish brat and always wanted the best for himself, and it got him in a peck of trouble. Abraham was always going off to rescue Lot from his latest escapade. They should have left him in Ur!

Abraham was greatly worried that he had no heir to whom he would leave his fortune and blessing. Sarah decided she would fix the situation, and that is where the Hagar debacle happened. That horror followed Sarah the rest of her life. It never occurred to her that she might be the one to provide Abraham an heir. Seriously? She was 90 years old. Those kinds of things just do not happen to women her age. Do they?

The thing that likely caused Sarah the most gray in her hair and wrinkles on her face, however, was the time when Abraham nearly sacrificed Isaac to the Lord. This was their only child and the child of their old age. Sarah thought it a bit weird when Abe loaded up the donkeys, the servants and Isaac and headed out to who-knows-where to offer a sacrifice. However, ole Abe was getting on up there in age, and she just assumed he was having a moment, so she did not ask any questions. Big mistake! It was a blessing she did not know what he was up to beforehand. I'm not sure her heart would have agreed to the plan, even if it was from God. Just saying…

Yes, Sarah certainly deserves some sort of award for patience and endurance in my book.

Today, let's narrow our focus to the one frame in God's Hall of Faith that focuses on Sarah and find out what really pleased God about her—what caused God to esteem her as a woman of great faith.

Please write out **Hebrews 11:11-12** in the space below, then underline the portion of the verses that gives us evidence of faith on Sarah's part. If possible, please write it out from either the New American Standard version or the New King James version.

_____

_____

_____

_____

I asked you to use specific versions of the Bible because those two highlight Sarah as a conduit of faith in God. Other translations, such as the NIV and NLT, highlight Abraham's faith. For the purposes of our study today, I want us to focus on Sarah. When I asked you to underline the portion of the verses that give evidence of Sarah's faith act, did you underline the part that spoke of Sarah judging God faithful to keep His promises? Turn to **Genesis 18** and read **verses 1-15**. Now that you have read the account of Sarah, please answer the following questions:

For context please turn back to **Genesis 17:1-2** and note what God had promised to Abraham when Abraham was 99 years old (several years after the Hagar mess).

_____

_____

Also in **Genesis 17:8**, God promised Abraham something other than descendants. What was it?

_____

_____

Sarah was mentioned in **Genesis 17.** What details are given specifically in **verse 16 and 19?**

_____

_____

Just to make sure we understand the enormity of what takes place, recall with me that Sarah and Abraham were well past childbearing age. Things just don't work well, or at all, when one is 90 or 99 years old, if you know what I mean. In addition to all that, even when Sarah had been of child-bearing age, she had been unable to conceive. So it is a gross understatement to say that things were not looking good for Abraham and Sarah ever having children. Ever!

As we look into chapter 18, we find some surprise visitors arriving at Abraham and Sarah's tent. As was the custom of the day, Abraham invited the visitors in and offered them some water with which to wash their feet and some food. It would have been considered an affront to talk business before the visitors had refreshed themselves.

Finally in **Genesis 18:9** the visitors reveal the purpose of their visit.

Who does the Bible make it seem they were there to see?

_____

This is the point at which the Bible moves from talking about the visitors as "they" and instead refers to "He."

We must return to **Genesis 18:1** to discover who the "He" is. Note what you discover here.

_____

_____

Allow me to set up the scene for you. Abraham, with the assistance of Sarah and a young man in their employ, has welcomed three men into their home, washed their feet, and fed them. Now, Abraham and the men begin to talk business. Sarah, the typical woman with curiosity about to kill her, stands behind the tent flap just beyond where the men are sitting. She wants to know why they have come and has no intention of missing a word that is spoken.

Suddenly, Sarah hears _her name_ again. They ask where she is. Oh my, what is this about? No one is ever interested in a woman unless they want her to do something for them. Her heart begins to beat faster.

What they say next causes her to laugh. In fact, she laughs so hard she has tears running down her face and has a really hard time being quiet with her laughter. That man just told her husband that this time next year she, Sarah, would be holding a baby boy that she had given birth to. She is 90 years old! Talk about Rolling On The Floor Laughing (ROTFL)! If it hadn't been so outlandishly funny, it would have made her cry tears of regret because she would never know the joy of being a mother.

Perhaps Sarah thought to herself, "Mister, did you fall and hit your head at some point? Don't you realize I am 90 years old? And have you even looked at Abraham? Things don't work anymore. There is no way humanly possible!"

What happens next is something that Sarah would never forget as long as she lived. The man looks Abraham right in the eye and says, "Why did Sarah laugh when I said that? Is anything too hard for God?"

You see, "humanly possible" is vastly different than "divinely possible." Sarah was operating only in the human realm, forgetting that the God they served was capable of more than they could ask or imagine.

Suddenly, and without thinking, Sarah gives herself away as she jumps to defend herself. She says, "I did not laugh."

The man says, "Yes, you did."

The Bible gives no indication that Sarah continued her flawed defense. We are left to wonder exactly what happened. Did the fact that the man knew exactly what had gone on in Sarah's mind bring forth a realization that she was in the same room with a messenger from God? Was there doubt in Sarah's heart that God could or would do what this man said He would do? What did Abraham say? Did Sarah ask any more questions? At what point did she believe?

We need more. We are people who want details. Yet, God chose not to give them to us. We know that everything happened just as God promised.

What does **Genesis 21:1** tell us that will encourage us in our faith walks?

_____

_____

_____

_____

The Lord did as He had said. Sarah had a son whom she named Isaac. Isaac became the father of Jacob, whose name was changed to Israel. He was the patriarch of the twelve tribes of Israel, and from the tribe of Judah would come the Messiah, Jesus Christ. The ultimate sacrifice to cover sin would be made by Jesus, the descendant of Abraham and Sarah. While Isaac was the child of the promise, Jesus was the Promise of God. God kept His promise to Abraham and Sarah, and every Jewish person who has ever been born is a descendant of Abraham.

In spite of the fact that the prophecy was beyond belief and so outlandish it begged for a laugh, Sarah, in faith, believed that God was able to do as He promised.

What circumstance in your life is begging for a little bit of Sarah-type faith? What is God asking of you that you just have to laugh at because it is not humanly possible? Is it a circumstance that is crazier than a 90-year-old getting pregnant and having a baby? What promise of God is intertwined in your situation? You may throw your head back and laugh at the absurdity of it, but when you have finished your laugh, I want to encourage you to believe that God is able to do what He has promised. If He has promised something, it will happen. Maybe not in your timeframe, but it will happen in God's timing. If God is asking something of you that seems impossible, please believe that He is able to bring to pass what He is asking. Stay faithful to the last word you heard from God. Believe Him for the impossible!

MEDITATION MOMENT:

John MacArthur says, "Faith sees the invisible, hears the inaudible, touches the intangible, and accomplishes the impossible." [39] Is there something invisible, inaudible, intangible or impossible in your life that needs some faith applied to it? Write about it below. When you have finished writing about it, let your final words on the page be "I believe."

_____

_____

_____

_____

_____

_____

Day 4 – By Faith...

I remember childhood birthdays and Christmases. First of all it seemed like they would never come around. Honestly, I think each year was a dozen years long when I was a young 'un. Birthdays and Christmases were preceded by a count-down to the big day. Oh, how slowly the time passed. By the time the celebration day arrived, my sister and I had nearly worked ourselves into a frenzy over the whole thing.

For me, those special occasions were as much about the food as they were about the gifts. Each year my birthday cake was made by Mrs. Vella Hughes, and it was the most delectable thing I put in my mouth all year long. She made a rich, creamy, three-layer vanilla cake with buttercream frosting that begged for a glass of cold milk to accompany it. I am a frosting girl…and a milk girl. Yes, I like the cake and will eat every bite of it, but frosting is what delights me. Oh sweet mercy, how I loved those cakes. I don't remember why I stopped having Mrs. Hughes' cakes or at what age. It could have been that my tastes changed, or perhaps Mrs. Hughes stopped making them. Whatever the reason, I would give a pretty penny for a piece of one of Mrs. Vella's cakes today.

Christmas did not have the food draw that birthdays offered. Nevertheless, there was a huge amount of anticipation that went along with it. My parents never splurged on my sister and me. Our gifts were heavily loaded with beautiful outfits handmade by my mother. It was always a treat to have a new outfit, and I was certain I would not meet anyone else on the street wearing the exact same thing. Mother did all her sewing while we were at school, so we never knew what our gifts would look like. We just knew they would be wonderful. I have great memories of opening gifts on Christmas morning and being so excited about everything I had been given. The dilemma was which new outfit I would wear first!

Eager anticipation! Confident expectation of something wonderful to come! We have all felt it in our lives. So did those whose lives are detailed for us in the Bible. How do we know? Let's dig a little deeper into Hebrews 11 and see what we can discover.

Two sets of verses will be our campsite today.

Read **Hebrews 11:1-13**. Note who the subjects of verse 13 are. In other words, who are the "these" the writer is speaking of?

_____

_____

_____

_____

Now take a look at **Hebrews 11:39** where we find another reference to "these." This is a different set of people than those referenced in verse 13. This group of people largely live in chapter 11 unnamed, with the exception of Isaac, Jacob, Joseph, Moses, Rahab, Gideon, Barak, Samson, Jephthah, David, and Samuel. Verses 33-38 are chock full of nameless examples of faith for us to ponder.

Today and tomorrow, however, we are going to turn our focus from the biblical examples of faith and begin writing our own "By Faith" stories. You and I will join the Hall of Faith and place a verse 41 at the end of chapter 11.

These two days will be quite different than anything we have done, previously, in our Hebrews study. But I believe they will allow us the opportunity to examine our faith walk, celebrate our victories, and tweak areas that need a bit of adjusting.

Let's begin by laying claim to some white space here on this page, and, if you dare, in your Bible. Over the course of two days, we will write out our faith journey, and we will do it using the very same words the writer of Hebrews chose… By Faith…

Please fill your name in the following blank.

41: "By faith, _____…"

Mine says, 41: "By faith, Leah…"

Now, if you have a mind to write in your Bible like I do, go to the end of Hebrews 11 and write exactly the phrase you just completed above.

We will divide our lives up into quarters for this exercise. How old are you today?

_____

Divide that number by 4: _____

This gives you the number of years in each quarter of your life. Today we will examine the first two quarters of our lives and begin to write our faith story. My example is provided below, just to be sure I have made my instructions clear.

Today I am 48 years old. 48 divided by 4 is 12. So today I will look for faith acts from birth-12 years old and 13-24 years of age. Tomorrow will take me from 25-36 years of age and 37-48 years old.

Make sense? Okay, let's get started. You will answer the same questions for each quarter of your life.

By Faith, _____ (your name)

First Quarter – Birth to Age_____

What significant events happened in this quarter of your life?

_____

_____

_____

_____

Who had a major impact (either positive or negative) on your faith in this period? What did they do or fail to do?

_____

_____

_____

_____

What were the greatest challenges to your faith during this part of your life?

_____

_____

_____

_____

How did you see God working in the midst of these challenges?

_____

_____

_____

_____

_____

What acts of faith do you think God would record in His Hall of Faith from this quarter of your life?

_____

_____

_____

_____

Write your "By Faith" statement here. Begin with…

"By faith, _____ (your name)" and then make a statement or statements about some faith step in this quarter of your life. Perhaps you want to write more than one. By all means, feel free.

Here is an example from my own life to help you get started.

By faith, Leah, when taken to church and taught the Scriptures during childhood, believed that God was Who He said He was and that what God said in the Bible was true.

Now, it is your turn.

_____

_____

_____

_____

_____

_____

_____

Second Quarter –

Age _____ to Age _____

What significant events happened in this quarter of your life?

_____

_____

_____

_____

_____

Who had a major impact (either positive or negative) on your faith in this period? What did they do or fail to do?

_____

_____

_____

_____

_____

What were the greatest challenges to your faith during this part of your life?

_____

_____

_____

_____

How did you see God working in the midst of these challenges?

_____

_____

_____

_____

_____

What acts of faith do you think God would record in His Hall of Faith from this quarter of your life?

_____

_____

_____

_____

_____

Write your "By Faith" statement here. Begin with "By faith, (your name)" and then make a statement or statements about some faith step in this quarter of your life. As before, feel free to write more than one.

_____

_____

_____

_____

_____

_____

_____

_____

_____

_____

_____

Great work! I know it is not an easy thing to do, but remembering what God has done in our lives is so important.

MEDITATION MOMENT:

Since you have done so much reflecting today, I'm going to give you a break. Tomorrow we will ponder the last two quarters of our lives.

Day 5 – More Faith Ponderings

Sometimes it only takes one act of faith, be it great or small, to trigger something unique and wonderful.

Early in the fifth century, in 404 AD, a Turkish monk named Telemachus ended up in Rome at one of the bloody gladiatorial contests. He was so offended by the contest and the senseless bloodshed that he jumped into the arena, crying out "In the name of Jesus, stop!"

The blood-thirsty crowd was so enraged by this man who was attempting to deprive them of their sport that they picked up rocks and stoned Telemachus to death.

The Emperor at the time, Honorius, was a Christian, and he was so impressed by the selfless act of Telemachus that he quickly made a law that banned gladiatorial contests all through the Roman Empire.

One act of faith by Telemachus changed so much in the Roman world. By faith, Telemachus…

Today, we gaze back at the third and fourth quarters of our faith journey with the goal of pulling out faith acts and recording them as "by faith" statements. Don't be discouraged if you cannot immediately pull from memory a few faith acts. If you have walked with Jesus any length of time, you have a few faith acts in your history. Stop now and ask the Holy Spirit to help you recall them.

Ok, let's get started. We will follow the same pattern of questioning we used yesterday.

By Faith, (your name)_____

Age _____ to Age _____

What significant events happened in this quarter of your life?

_____

_____

_____

_____

Who had a major impact (either positive or negative) on your faith in this period? What did they do or fail to do?

_____

_____

_____

_____

_____

What were the greatest challenges to your faith during this part of your life?

_____

_____

_____

_____

_____

How did you see God working in the midst of these challenges?

_____

_____

_____

_____

_____

What acts of faith do you think God would record in His Hall of Faith from this quarter of your life?

_____

_____

_____

_____

_____

Write your "By Faith" statement here. Begin with "By faith, (your name)" and then make a statement or statements about some faith step in this quarter of your life. As in yesterday's assignment, please feel free to write more than one.

_____

_____

_____

_____

_____

_____

_____

_____

_____

Fourth Quarter

Age _____ to Age _____

What significant events happened in this quarter of your life?

_____

_____

_____

_____

Who had a major impact (either positive or negative) on your faith in this period? What did they do or fail to do?

_____

_____

_____

_____

What were the greatest challenges to your faith during this part of your life?

_____

_____

_____

_____

_____

How did you see God working in the midst of these challenges?

_____

_____

_____

_____

_____

What acts of faith do you think God would record in His Hall of Faith from this quarter of your life?

_____

_____

_____

_____

_____

Write your "By Faith" statement here. Begin with…

"By faith, _____ (your name)" and then make a statement or statements about some faith step in this quarter of your life.

Have you guessed that you can write more than one?

_____

_____

_____

_____

_____

Once again, you have done some good work. I hope these two days have proven beneficial to you and have given you reasons to rejoice in what the Lord has done in your life to this day. I'm thinking of the verse in 1 Samuel 7:12 where Samuel sets up a stone between Mizpah and Shem, named it Ebenezer, and declared, "Thus far the Lord has helped us." Over the past two days, you have set up stones of remembrance, stones of faith. Today, you can confidently declare, "Thus far the Lord has helped me."

MEDITATION MOMENT:

Which of your personal "by faith" statements from the past two days has meant the most to you and why? Plan to share this with your small group.

May I Serve You?

Writing this Bible study has been a great reason to visit recipes that have not been used in a long time. Such is the case with this week's coffee cake recipe. I got it from a friend in the early 90's, used it a lot for several years, and have not made it in about 15 years. I don't know why I abandoned it, because it is delicious!

This Banana Coffee Cake is a great addition to a brunch or breakfast event. The cake is moist, flavorful, and delish! A cup of Caribou House Blend® Coffee would be a perfect complement to this delicacy.

RECIPE

BANANA COFFEE CAKE

Preheat oven to 350 degrees. Cream together and blend well:

1 ¼ cup sugar

½ cup butter

½ cup shortening

Add and blend well:

2 eggs

4 ripe, mashed bananas

1 teaspoon vanilla

5 tablespoons milk

Add and blend well:

2 cups cake flour

1 teaspoon baking soda

Grease and flour a 9 x 13 baking dish. Pour batter into dish.

Mix together and place on top of the cake batter:

¾ stick melted butter

Small can of coconut

¾ cup brown sugar

Bake at 350 degrees for 40 minutes. DO NOT OVERCOOK!

NOTE: Tastes better if made the day before serving.

Week 7 – In View of All This: The Now and Then Blend

As a girl in high school, I always loved pep rally days. The noise, the excitement, the school spirit, the cheerleaders, all seeking to encourage the team to be ready to win the big game…the whole thing was so thrilling. Hebrews 12 is a pep rally, of sorts. The cheerleader is the writer of Hebrews. The team is made up of every person who names Jesus as his or her Lord. We have a big game that we must show up for and play every day. The game requires faith, perseverance, sacrifice, goal setting, and determination. The prize is hearing "well done, good and faithful servant" from our Lord when we leave this earthly tent behind for the glories of heaven.

As we move into chapter 12 of the book of Hebrews, we find the writer switching gears. Up to this point in his sermon, he has focused on how faith in Jesus Christ is far superior to the faith of the Jewish forefathers. Faith has been examined from both the Old Testament and New Testament points of view, and Jesus has been held up as the object of faith in chapters one through ten. Chapter 11 offered practical examples of how faith makes a difference in the life of a walking, talking, real live person. As we come to chapter twelve, the writer seems to prepare to wrap up his sermon by giving a practical pep talk to his listeners. Join me for the Hebrews pep rally!

Day 1 – The Cure for Spiritual ADHD

When I was a child in the 1970s, we had never heard of Attention Deficit Hyperactivity Disorder. No doubt, some of my classmates could have been poster children for the problem, but it had yet to be named as such. The cure for the problem in those days was not a drug, but a paddle and strict discipline in the home and at school. Both solutions worked well in most situations.

Attention Deficit Hyperactivity Disorder is described by the National Institute of Mental Health's website in the following way: "Attention Deficit Hyperactivity Disorder is one of the most common childhood disorders and can continue through adolescence and adulthood. Symptoms include difficulty staying focused and paying attention, difficulty controlling behavior, and hyperactivity (over-activity)." [40]

I think the author of Hebrews had been given a glimpse into the need of his Christian church members to overcome their spiritual ADHD in order to run the faith race well. As we have learned, they likely were being persecuted for their faith, so they were probably having trouble staying focused on the faith race. Some may have gone back to the old works-based system of Judaism, while others may have abandoned the faith altogether. Spiritual ADHD.

Let's look at the first two verses of **Hebrews 12**, as we seek the cure for this faith-destroying illness. These are two verses I memorized early in my faith walk, and they have been used by God repeatedly to encourage and challenge me. I hope our focused look at them today begins the process of cementing them in your heart and mind.

I am taking **verse 1** from the *New Century Version* (NCV) and **verse 2** from the New Living Translation (NLT) because I like the wording:

1. *We are surrounded by a great cloud of people whose lives tell us what faith means. So let us run the race that is before us and never give up. We should remove from our lives anything that would get in the way and the sin that so easily holds us back.*

2. *We do this by keeping our eyes on Jesus, the champion who initiates and perfects our faith. Because of the joy awaiting him, he endured the cross, disregarding its shame. Now he is seated in the place of honor beside God's throne.*

In short, these verses tell us three things:

1. Others came before us and ran a great faith race.

2. We can run a great faith race.

3. Keep our focus on Jesus.

We have already considered the first of these three reminders in our study time last week. Today, let's delve into the second and third points.

You can run a great faith race…using a few tips!

The writer uses an athletic competition theme to encourage his audience, and they would have understood this perfectly. Picture a relay race. There are multiple runners, and after each has run a lap, they carefully hand a baton off to the next runner. Dropping the baton means almost certain defeat in the race.

Past generations have run the faith race…Abraham, Moses, Paul, the Wesley brothers, Timothy Dwight, Charles Spurgeon, Amy Carmichael, Dwight L. Moody, Billy Graham, Kay Arthur, and Beth Moore. They ran and ran well. Now the baton is being handed off to you and me. What must we do in order to run well?

Look back at **Hebrews 12:1 (NCV)** and complete the following sentences:

- *So let us run the race that is before us and _____*
_____ _____. We should
_____ from our _____ any-
thing that would _____ _____ _____
_____ and the _____ that so easily holds us back.

Get rid of what hinders! Never give up! Let's look at both of these for a moment.

Get rid of what hinders!

As I researched the meaning of the Greek words used in this passage, one struck me as worthy of mention. It seems to be a fairly innocuous word, but in it, I believe, is hidden the key to getting rid of what hinders us.

Verse 2 tells us to get rid of, in general, anything that gets in the way of our faith walk. Anything means anything! Whatever is an obstacle to your faith race needs to go. What presents an obstacle to you might not be an obstacle to me. For one it might be pornography, while for another the obstacle might be Facebook or Twitter. For one the obstacle could be a friendship, while for another it might be money. There are as many obstacles to faith as there are people. The key is to identify your obstacle.

Would you take a few moments, pray, and ask the Lord to reveal to you any obstacles, any hindrances, to your faith. It may be a good thing, but not a God thing. Don't rule out anything. Please take time to do this. As the Lord reveals hindrances to you, list them here. We will return to this in a moment.

_____

_____

The author of Hebrews then goes on to be very specific about one thing that hinder us: sin—disobedience to God—doing what we know is outside of God's revealed will.

I don't think I have to expound on sin. Whether you freely admit it or not, you know what sin looks like in your life. You may try to deny it, but deep within your heart, you know when you sin. Now, go back to the space above and add to the list any sin the Holy Spirit brings to your mind. Perhaps you need to use abbreviations or code words to make the list if it is something that needs to remain between you and God. Whatever you have to do to make the list…just do it!

Now, the key to getting rid of what hinders! The Greek word used for getting rid of is *apotithemi,* and it means, "to lay aside, get rid of, do away with." It is a verb and a verb, as we all learned in high school English class (thank you, Mrs. Myers), is an action word. It requires that we do something. The sin and hindrances to your faith journey and to my faith journey must be dealt with by each of us. I cannot deal with your hindrances, and you cannot deal with mine. Each of us must do the work of laying aside and getting rid of our hindrances and sin. Until we take that responsibility and do the hard thing, we will never have a great faith walk. We cannot hang onto our pet sin and expect to find our names in God's Hall of Faith. We must boldly confront them and refuse to give them a place in our lives!

In this moment you and I need to decide if we are serious about leaving a legacy of faith for those to whom we will pass the baton. If we are not willing to take the necessary actions to get rid of sin and hindrances in our lives, we are not ready to walk out a great faith journey. We cannot pass the baton of faith to the next generation until we deal with our sin.

Never give up!

Never give up. Even though you mess up, never give up. Keep on keeping on in the faith race. It will be hard. There will be times of discouragement. There will be people who tell you it is not worth it. Never give up! Never give up!! Never, never, never give up!

This brings us to the final portion of the cure for spiritual ADHD, and it is found in **Hebrews 12:2**.

Please look back at **verse 2** from the beginning of our lesson and write the first nine words below.

_____

_____

If my instructions were clear, you should have written: "We do this by keeping our eyes on Jesus."

I could use so many illustrations for this point, but I'm going with horses. Blinders are placed on horses to keep them focused on what is in front of them. Without the blinders, they get distracted by the things going on to the side and behind them. They lose their focus. Hebrews 12:2 encourages us to place blinders around our spiritual eyes so that all we can focus on is Jesus. We need to look straight ahead at Jesus.

Consider what would have happened if Jesus had gotten distracted from His mission of salvation. There were a thousand things that could have distracted Him:

• *His family—the pain His mother suffered at His crucifixion.*

• *His disciples—they might not be ready for Him to leave. What if they were not prepared to carry on His work?*

• *The sick and demon possessed—there were always more to be healed.*

• *The unsaved—there were always more He could interact with.*

• *His own physical fatigue—there were probably many times He just wanted to get away and rest.*

• *The potential glory of being a political king—the Jews were ready and eager for Him to establish an earthly, political reign.*

• *The pain of crucifixion and death—it was a horrendously awful way to die.*

Do you see what I mean? Any one of these things could have easily distracted the human side of Christ from His mission. Yet, He fixed His eyes on the prize at the end and did not allow Himself to become distracted.

Those of us who call ourselves Christian have a faith mission during our time on this spinning globe. Our mission is to make Jesus known. How easy it is to

become distracted and veer off course! I've done it, and I bet you have too. Now is the time; today is the day to commit to fixing our eyes on Jesus and staying the course of faith. Will you? Only you can make that decision.

MEDITATION MOMENT:

Let's end today with a question…or two. Make these a matter of prayer and reflection between you and God.

- Are you faithfully walking out your mission of making Jesus known to those who circle around your life?

- When is the last time you shared with someone else what Jesus has done in your life?

- What obstacles and distractions are hindering you from your faith mission?

- Are you willing to fix your eyes squarely on Jesus, to get rid of the distractions and hindrances in order to do what you were placed here to do?

Day 2 — Discipline: It's Because I Love You

When my sister and I were growing up, our parents did not hesitate to discipline us, and we learned early that rebellion earned us a spanking we did not soon forget. We were not abused, and the spankings did not damage our self-esteem. In fact, they gave us a healthy respect for authority. My personal opinion is that spankings are not used nearly often enough today.

Our daddy did most of the spanking, and when Daddy administered a spanking, you knew you had been spanked. Daddy had polio when he was 16 years old, and for the rest of his life, he walked with crutches, which made his arms and shoulders very, very strong. So, when he paddled us, there was no doubt in our minds that we had been spanked! Trust me, spankings were huge deterrents for me against rebellion and disobedience, at least as a child.

I recall one day when my sister got a spanking from Daddy. Our Aunt Janie was visiting that day and she and Mother happened to be sitting in close proximity to the spanking. I think Janie was completely traumatized by what took place.

Leslie had disobeyed, and Daddy told her to get in the bedroom. He got the Bolo Paddle (anyone remember those?) out of the drawer, followed her into the bedroom, and closed the door.

The door had no sooner latched when Leslie began crying and screaming at the top of her lungs. I'm telling you, people a mile away could have heard her.

"No! **Please** don't spank me! Oh! No! **Please** don't spank me! I won't do that again!"

As the screams continued, Aunt Janie turned to Mother with a horrified look on her face and said, "Bobbie, make him stop. He is hurting her. Do something!"

Mother, with a knowing look, said, "Janie, he hasn't even touched her yet!"

The very thought of discipline brought out the screamer in my sister. I always wondered if it ever occurred to her that the scream probably made the discipline worse.

Some Christian circles like to focus exclusively on the love and goodness of God, and He *is* loving and good. What those same people conveniently forget is that God is also just and righteous, and He cannot and will not tolerate sin and disobedience in His children. Nowhere in the Scriptures is God's love disconnected from His justice and righteousness. In fact, anytime justice and judgment was

meted out toward a person or people, it was done only after they were given ample warning and opportunity to make a change.

God's character never changes. Even today when God disciplines His children, it is only after He has given us warnings and opportunities to make different choices. Let's look at Hebrews 12 as we consider this issue of godly discipline.

Read **Hebrews 12:3-13** and note the number of times the words discipline, punishment, chastening, or other synonyms are used.

_____

The repetition of the word discipline in this short passage is significant because God wants us to understand the importance of His discipline. Today, let's focus on two questions:

1.   What is the purpose of God's discipline?

2.   How are we to react to God's discipline?

What is the purpose of God's discipline?

I believe we find the answers to this question in three verses within this passage. Read the following verses and note the purpose of God's discipline.

12:7-8 –

_____

_____

12:9 –

_____

_____

12:11 –

_____

_____

I hope you found the three purposes of God's discipline:

• _to confirm that we are God's child_

• _to teach us respect for Jehovah God_

• _to bring forth righteousness in us_

166

Let's take a quick peek at each one.

To confirm that we are God's child

Part of the responsibility of parents is the appropriate discipline of their child—not the neighbor's child or the child of anyone else, but their own child. Disciplining a child when he or she has been rebellious is the way to bring the child into conformity with the parent's expectations for behavior. In the same way, God has expectations for the behavior of His children, and when we misbehave, He has every right to discipline us. That discipline shows that we belong to Him and that He loves us.

How does **Proverbs 13:24** confirm this?

_____

To teach us respect for Jehovah God

There are several reasons we should respect God. Let's glance at a few. Read the verse and note the reason God deserves our respect:

Genesis 1:1

_____

_____

Deuteronomy 11:26-28

_____

_____

Job 12:9-10

_____

_____

Psalm 139:13

_____

_____

Proverbs 2:6

_____

_____

Romans 5:8

_____

_____

Revelation 21:1-4

_____

_____

There is no shortage of reasons why we should give honor and respect to God. The simple fact that He is GOD should be reason enough. This is a bit like when we were children and we asked our parents "Why?" about a particular issue. Their response may very well have been, "Because I am the parent and I said so." That was sufficient.

To bring forth righteousness in us

God disciplines us so we will be right before God. Sin and rebellion make us out of sorts with God because He is perfect and holy. Discipline seeks to bring us back to right standing before God. It hopefully makes us realize that we have strayed from the right way and encourages us to change. When we are living in righteousness, we will act more like Jesus, talk more like Jesus, and think more like Jesus. On our own, and without discipline for our rebellion, you and I would never conform to the image of Christ. _Never!_

Now that we have examined the purposes for discipline, let's consider how we are to react to discipline. The following two quotes help us understand the proper response to God's discipline.

The first is a quote from James Montgomery Boice from _Nehemiah: An Expositional Commentary_. Boice says the following:

"Many people…do not show growth in their walks with Jesus Christ because they do not want to change the way they are living. At times they might even be moved to tears by their failures. But they do not surge ahead because basically they want to do exactly as they have been doing." [41]

Well, well, well, now. That is pretty much where the rubber hits the proverbial road, isn't it? You and I want either our way or God's way. This is not Burger King. You cannot have it your way. In order to be right with God, we must do things HIS way. Period. The issue is not up for discussion. So, either we respond to discipline and do life God's way, or we ignore discipline and pay the steep and heavy consequences for disobedience.

Some may say, "Well, I've been doing it my way for a while, and nothing has happened to me."

To that I say, "Nothing has happened to you, YET."

There will be a price for disobedience. Paul is painfully clear on this point.

Write **Galatians 6:7** here.

_____

_____

_____

_____

_____

The decision is yours, friend. If God is disciplining you over a matter, make it easy on yourself and respond to that discipline in humility and repentance. You won't be sorry.

Now, to the second quote. Not only should we respond to discipline in humility, but we need to respond immediately. Consider this quote from Arthur Pink:

"Remind yourself of how much dross there is yet among the gold and view the corruption of your own heart and marvel that God has not smitten you more severely. Form the habit of heeding His taps, and you will be less likely to receive His raps." [42]

What is Pink saying? The very second you feel that twinge of conviction or conscience is the second to do something about it. Avoid the discipline of God, if at all possible. As I said at the beginning of today's lesson, God never disciplines without giving ample warning and time to make a change. The time to make a change is _before_ God has to discipline you. Heed His taps so you won't receive His raps!

Friends, God does not discipline you because he enjoys it. It does not make Him feel powerful and big, despite the fact that He _is_ powerful and big. He disciplines because He desires the best for you. He does it for the same reason you discipline your child. He LOVES you. He loves YOU!

MEDITATION MOMENT:

Is there an area of your life where God is tapping you on the shoulder and saying, "Excuse me. Don't you think you need to make a change here?" How are you responding to that? Are you heeding His tap in order to avoid His rap, or is He bringing discipline your way because you ignored the tap? It is never too late to make a change and get in line with the way God wants you to live. Spend some time journaling here about these questions and your answers to them.

Day 3 – Believer or Non-Believer?

Today we take a trip back into the very center of the book of Hebrews to cover material I purposely delayed covering until now. While the topic may initially seem out of context with the rest of the week, I don't think it is. Hebrews 5:12—6:12 is one of the most difficult passages in the Bible to understand. Biblical scholars fall on each end of the spectrum in their thoughts and opinions on this passage. I tried to figure out a way we could study Hebrews without having to consider this group of verses, but it is impossible. Hebrews is thirteen chapters and chapter six kind of falls right in the middle of them all. I've decided to simply offer you not only what scholars say, but what I believe God wants us to learn as we study the passage. So, lace up your hiking boots, and let's walk into Hebrews 6.

Have you ever written a letter, email, or text and thought you were perfectly clear about the information you desired to convey, only to have the recipient end up confused and not understanding what you said? I have, and it can be so frustrating. As a speaker and a writer, I diligently try to make everything I convey clear and understandable. After I published the first Bible study in the Legacy series, *From the Trash Pile to the Treasure Chest: Creating a Godly Legacy*, I had the opportunity to walk through the study with a group from my church. One particular matching exercise in the study proved to be a bit more involved and taxing for the group than I had anticipated. In fact, for some, it was downright confusing. At that point, it did not matter that it made perfect sense to me. My students and readers were having trouble with it. I had put hours of work into making the study user-friendly, yet one part of it was not. How frustrating!

I think if the writer of Hebrews lived among us today, he or she might feel much the same way. He knew what he was trying to convey to his readers, but those of us who live thousands of years this side of the cross and the culture of that day are walking around confused about the sixth chapter. As I have prayed about how to tackle this passage, the Lord has encouraged me to adopt the Apostle Paul's view and say to you, "I do not want you ignorant, friends." So, what we will do is bring in some experts to help us with the material. This chapter of Hebrews offers us an opportunity to visit with some esteemed biblical scholars and hear their thoughts about this highly debated section of Scripture. Although I do not fall into the category of "esteemed biblical scholar," I will offer you what my heart tells me about this segment as we go through it.

I ask you to consider prayerfully all the opinions offered, then race straight to the Holy Spirit and ask Him to show you what all of this means. He is the

only accurate interpreter of Scripture, and He will guide you into all truth. Honestly, when it comes to difficult passages like this, I try to remember that my salvation does NOT hinge on whether I totally understand this passage. I encourage you to remember that. All too often we are just downright ugly to others who do not agree with our opinions. While the issues of salvation and growing in the faith are foundational, the issues concerning the passage itself are considered less foundational.

In our focal passage, the writer is encouraging his readers to grow up in the faith. He urges them to become mature and not remain spiritual babies. It is with this background that we jump in today.

Begin by reading the focal passage in **Hebrews 5:12—Hebrews 6:12**.

List every adjective the author uses to describe his readers in this passage.

_____

_____

_____

_____

Now list the things from this passage the author says should be part of the life of a mature believer.

_____

_____

_____

_____

Finally, list the things the author considers elementary teachings about Christ from **Hebrews 6:1-2**.

_____

_____

_____

_____

_____

I think it would be beneficial for us to do a little review so that we will have this passage in context. The book of Hebrews contains much information about the customs and practices of the Jewish people living under the Old Covenant. The author's readers would have had to be familiar with very detailed Jewish concepts like Moses, Melchizedek, the priests, the Old Covenant, the sacrifices, and the tabernacle. So, it is safe to assume that many, if not most, of his readers were Jewish in origin. In addition, in chapters one and two, he offered an in-depth discussion of Jesus and the salvation found only in Him. In Hebrews 4, the author seems to be including his readers in the "we" and "us" when he says in verse 14, "seeing then that we have a great High Priest who has passed through the heavens, Jesus the Son of God, let US hold fast our confession" [emphasis added]. This occurs many times in the book of Hebrews (8:1-2; 10:19-27; 12:1-3) and seems to signify that the author considers his readers to have placed saving faith in Jesus at some point in the past.

This is the point where we find the "rub" among scholars. To what kind of audience was the author of Hebrews speaking? Were they solely a group of Jews, or were there Gentiles in their midst? Were they believers who were in danger of returning to the old ways of Judaism, or were they unbelievers who were regular attendees of the house church? Honestly, there are reasonable arguments to support both viewpoints regarding the spiritual state of the audience, and I hope to walk you through a few of those. For the rest of today and tomorrow, let's take a section at a time and look at some of the compelling opinions on each side. This kind of studying is very helpful in learning to discern the Word.

First we will look at **Hebrews 5:12-14**. Read it in your Bible, please.

Warren Wiersbe in his marvelous commentary on Hebrews entitled, *Be Confident: Live by Faith, Not by Sight*, interprets the recipients of the book of Hebrews as believing Jews who are in danger of backsliding. He equates "milk" with the work of Jesus while on earth and "meat" or "solid food" with the work that Jesus now does in heaven on behalf of the believer. Those who are spiritually immature have taken advantage of the milk—the "birth, life, teaching, death, burial, and resurrection" of Jesus, but have not progressed on in their sanctification or spiritual growth. [43]

Word Biblical Commentary (WBC) also asserts that the audience is comprised of believers who are mature. Consider the following thoughts:

> "The writer shows no inclination to review with his hearers the foundational elements of the Christian faith. He clearly regarded the hearers as mature." [44]

173

WBC goes on to say: "The immediate intention is to shame them into recognizing that they are mature and must assume the responsibilities that accrue to a spiritually mature group of Christians in a hostile society.

"What the writer actually believes his intended readers to be is expressed by the image of the adult, and this is confirmed by the solid food they have received, and continue to receive in the homily.

"The signs of regression they have displayed are an abberational innovation that marred their integrity and imperiled their spiritual welfare." [45]

Because *Word Biblical Commentary* is a more scholarly commentary, I want to make sure we are all on the same page with their thoughts. WBC asserts that the believers are a group of established Christians who have received solid biblical teaching by the author of Hebrews in chapters 1—5, as well as in chapters 7—13. They are being reprimanded for simply getting lazy in their walk with Christ.

Hmm, getting lazy in their walk with Christ. Sound familiar? Perhaps these Hebrews needed a dose of Paul's encouragement from **Philippians 3:12 (NIV1984).**

Fill in the blanks from this well known verse:
Not that I have already _____ *all this,*
or have already _____ _____
_____ _____ _____, *but I*
_____ _____ *to take hold of that for*
which Christ Jesus took hold of me.

John MacArthur, in his commentary on Hebrews, gives a very different perspective when he says,

> "the maturity being called for is not that of a Christian's growing in the faith, but of an unbeliever's coming into the faith—into full-grown, mature truths and blessings of the New Covenant." [46]

He goes on to say,

> "For the time and study they have put in, they ought to be teachers of the Word of God. But they do not even comprehend its fundamentals. They have been 'advanced' students of Scripture for decades, and yet they do not even know Jesus Christ." [47]

MacArthur likens the Old Covenant to the alphabet that is taught to kindergarteners, while the New Covenant is the full message. The Jews being addressed had become dull to even their Old Covenant principles, the basic ABCs of their faith. These unbelieving Jews had heard the story of Christ and of all He offered through the New Covenant so many times they should have been able to teach it, but because they had never truly accepted Christ, they still needed the basics, the alphabet. Likewise, the mature believer would have been able to discern good and evil, while the unbelieving person could not.

MacArthur's position is very different from the first two mentioned, yet it is defensible, as you can see. Tomorrow we will consider Hebrews 6:1-12 in the same way in which we have examined Hebrews 5:12-14 today. God is not the author of confusion, and He desires for you to understand the Scriptures. I encourage you to ask the Holy Spirit to enlighten your mind to the truth of God's Word.

MEDITATION MOMENT:

One of the hallmark signs of a mature believer is to be able to rightly divide the Word and to discern truth. Considering the background you have studied up to now and our brief discussion of Hebrews 5:12-14, jot down your thoughts about what you believe concerning the audience to whom the writer of Hebrews is writing.

Day 4 – Seeking Truth in Hebrews 6

Today, as we study God's Word together, I want us to dive into Hebrews 6. But first, because this material is difficult to understand, let's take a moment to ask the Holy Spirit to guide our study.

Dear Lord, we understand You are not the author of confusion. Would You please enlighten our minds and hearts to receive from Hebrews 6 exactly what You desire for us to learn? Help us to open our hearts and allow the Holy Spirit free access to teach and guide us to truth. In the strong name of Jesus we ask these prayers. Amen!

In these twelve verses we find more discussion about elementary teachings. We also run into the issue of falling away. Hebrews 6:6 is one of the key verses used to support the position of those who believe we can lose our salvation. We will divide today's study of Hebrews 6 into three parts and consider what a few scholars have to say about them. I hope that you, with the help of the Holy Spirit, will formulate what you believe about each of these verses.

The first set of verses we will consider is **Hebrews 6:1-6**. Please read them in your Bible.

There are two key issues in this set of verses—the first being what the writer meant when he talked of "elementary teachings" in verse one. The second issue is that of "falling away" referenced in verse 6. Let's consider some opinions on this most difficult of passages.

The truths listed in verses 1 and 2 are what the writer is referencing when he talks of elementary teachings. Warren Wiersbe believes these to be basic teachings of both the Old and New Covenants, i.e. Judaism and Christianity. He says that the first two (repentance and faith) are directed toward God and signal the beginning of the spiritual life; the second two (baptisms and laying on of hands) have to do with the believer's relationship with the body of Christ; the final two (resurrection and judgment) pertain to the future. Wiersbe says that the lesson of these first three verses is "You have laid the foundation. You know your ABCs. Now move forward! Let God carry you along to maturity!"[48] *Word Biblical Commentary* shares much the same belief as Wiersbe on these verses.

John MacArthur's opinion is different from both Wiersbe and *Word Biblical Commentary*. He states that while the six truths are elementary or central to the Old Covenant or Judaism, they are not to New Covenant Christianity. They point to Christ and the gospel but are not part of the gospel. Consider MacArthur's synopsis of these verses: "The point of Hebrews 6:1-2 is simply that the unbelieving Jews should let go completely of the immature, elementary shadows and symbols of the Old Covenant and take hold of the mature and perfect reality of the New. The Holy Spirit is calling for them to leave the ABCs of **repentance from dead works** for the New Testament teaching of repentance toward God and new life in Christ. Leave the ABCs of **faith toward God** for faith in the Person of Jesus Christ. Leave the ABCs of **ceremonial washings** for the cleansing of the soul by the Word. Leave the ABCs of **laying hands** on the sacrifice for laying hold of the Lamb of God by faith. Leave the ABCs of the **resurrection of the dead** for the full and glorious resurrection unto life. Leave the ABCs of **eternal judgment** for the full truth of judgment and rewards as revealed in the New Covenant." [49]

Take a moment to consider these opinions and jot down any thoughts that come to you regarding verses 1-3 in the space below.

Editors' Note: Regarding Hebrews 6:4-6: "Many Christians do not share the view in the following eight (8) paragraphs because the text can be translated in several different ways. The *NIV Study Bible* says, "This is one long, complicated sentence in the Greek text. Its difficulties have led to many interpretations. However these verses are interpreted, their original purpose was to motivate the first readers to faithfulness in the face of persecution or pressure…. The Greek word for 'fall away' in verse 6 implies a willful and purposeful decision to reject Christ. Repentance is impossible for persons who make such a choice. This is not referring to unwitting sins but to sins committed in willful defiance of God (see 10:26). The clause translated 'because… they are crucifying the Son of God all over again' is often translated 'while' (rather than "because"). This suggests that repentance may not be 'impossible' forever but that it absolutely can never happen while a person is in a state of rebellion against God." [1] (This is the Wesleyan/Armenian view of Hebrews 6.)

---

[1] *Reflecting God Study Bible*, Kenneth Barker, ed. (Grand Rapids, MI: Zondervan Publishing House, 2000), 1863n

Now let's turn to the issue of falling away. Keep in mind the FINISHED work of Christ on the cross (Hebrews 7:26-27) and the fact that He SAT down at the right hand of God when the work was done (Hebrews 8:1). Please glance back and re-read **Hebrews 6:4-6** to refresh your memory.

Verses 4 and 5 describe a group of people or persons in general. It is unclear whether the author of Hebrews was speaking in generalities in these two verses or if he was pointing a finger at his audience as if to say, "This describes you." We simply do not know.

The other great unknown in this set of verses is what exactly the author meant by "fall away." Does this phrase "fall away" mean apostasy (renouncing the faith) or not? Did he really mean one could lose his or her salvation? Let's tap the minds of our scholars and find out what they think.

Expositor's Bible Commentary puts forth the opinion that these verses deal with apostasy from the Christian faith or even making progress in the faith. These commentators explain the meaning of "fall away" in verse 6 as saying that the author of Hebrews does not say the people described in verses 4 and 5 "cannot be forgiven or cannot be restored to salvation."

They believe that the author had repentance in mind and that when a person backslides from the faith, "such a person cannot bring himself or herself to this repentance." [50] Only God can.

Warren Wiersbe offers an understandable and quite reasonable explanation of these verses in *Be Confident*. He first explains that the word used for "fall away" in verse six is not the Greek word, *apostasia,* but rather, *parapipto,* which means, "to fall alongside." [51] In addition, Wiersbe offers several verses in the Bible that assure the believer that he or she cannot lose salvation. Some of the best are the verses that follow verse 6 which we will look at a bit later. Let's take a look at a few of these.

Read the following verses and paraphrase what they tell us.

John 5:24

_____

_____

_____

_____

John 10:27-30

_____

_____

_____

_____

Romans 8:28-39

_____

_____

_____

_____

_____

Wiersbe believes that the writer of Hebrews was "describing a hypothetical case to prove his point that a true believer cannot lose his salvation." He goes on to explain: "Let's suppose that you do not go on to maturity. Does this mean that you will go back to condemnation, that you will lose your salvation? Impossible! If you _could_ lose your salvation, it would be impossible to get it back again; and this would disgrace Jesus Christ. He would have to be crucified again for you, and this could never happen." [52]

John MacArthur, on the other hand, believes that Christians are not the intended audience of the letter to the Hebrews, so it is the opportunity for _receiving_ salvation that is being addressed here. MacArthur does not believe that Christians can lose their salvation, and he uses the passages from John 10 and Romans 8 that we studied above as a reference for his belief. He goes on to say, "If the power of God cannot keep us, nothing is dependable or trustworthy or worth believing in." [53]

Dear student of God's Word, I believe the work Jesus did on the cross is permanent and completely able to keep us forever. We are secure for all eternity. The problem in all this is the free will that God gave you and me. We can choose, at any time, to walk away from God, but that does not mean He will walk away from us. Once we belong to Him, He never leaves us or forsakes us. We are always His…the problem is that He may not always be ours. That is our choice.

Now, let's turn to **verses 7 and 8 of Hebrews chapter 6**. These two verses almost seem out of place in the context of this chapter until you really study them. Read them again.

The author of Hebrews uses an analogy of the land to compare those people who hear the gospel and accept it with those who hear it, yet reject it. Those who hear and accept the gospel produce fruit "in keeping with repentance," while those who hear and reject the gospel produce fruit in keeping with their sinfulness. The rejection of the gospel and the saving work of Jesus by any person will result in eternal disaster. The focus of these two verses is on the fruit produced as a result of choices made.

Perhaps this is a good time to remind ourselves of the fruit that we, as Christ followers, should be producing. Turn to **Galatians 5:22-23** and list below the fruit you find in these verses. As you write them out, consider how these fruit are evident in your life.

_____

_____

_____

_____

_____

Let's finish this day of study by examining **Hebrews 6:9-12**. Please read it in your Bible. I know this is difficult material and you may feel like you are in a seminary class, but if it were not important, God would not have included it in His Word, so persevere, my friend.

The author of Hebrews winds up this intense section of his message, or homily, by offering an encouraging word to his audience. He does this by reminding them that God has not forgotten the good works they have done in the name of the Lord in the past. He also encourages them to not grow sluggish or lazy in doing these good works.

What does **2 Chronicles 16:9a** add to this word of encouragement for you and me?

_____

_____

_____

_____

Expositor's Bible Commentary has this to say about Hebrews 6:9-12: "…the Christian profession of the readers had been more than formal, and they had shown in changed lives what that profession meant. This, the writer is saying, would not go unnoticed with God."[54]

The writer bases his conviction of their salvation on the fact that they had produced fruit in keeping with repentance in the past, and he desires that they not grow weary, but continue to follow the Lord wholeheartedly in the future.

My guess is that there is not a single one of us who has not grown weary of running the Christian race at some point in our past. I know I have. Life is busy and often difficult. Perhaps you are at that place right now, where it seems like you take one step forward in your Christian walk only to be knocked back two steps by the devil. Everything seems to go wrong all at the same time. You are discouraged and just cannot understand why God is allowing the things to happen in your life that you are experiencing. You thought God promised you one thing, yet something completely different has transpired. You feel like you have more to give than God is allowing you to offer at this time…more talent, more ability. I understand, and so does God.

Let's finish up by using our Meditation Moment to hear God's heart on this issue of growing weary and discouraged.

MEDITATION MOMENT:

Look up the following verses and write out what they speak to your heart. Be encouraged, my friend, God has not forgotten you.

Ecclesiastes 3:1-8

_____

_____

_____

Lamentations 3:22-23

_____

_____

Isaiah 43:1-3

_____

_____

Day 5 – World Peace or Whirled Peas?

In the 1990s there was a popular bumper sticker that read: "Visualize World Peace." I heard about a family driving behind a car with one of these world peace bumper stickers on the back of their car. The parents were commenting on the bumper sticker, and in the course of the conversation had read the words out loud. Their young son was sitting in the backseat, seemingly not paying attention to the parents' conversation in the front seat.

After a few minutes the parents grew quiet and the little boy piped up from the back, "Mom, what's so great about whirled peas? I don't even like peas."

Unfortunately, in today's world we are about as likely to see whirled peas as we are world peace.

Peace. Everyone wants it, but very few experience it. As I ponder the word, my immediate thought is "elusive." Peace seems so elusive in the world in which we live. Every day, somewhere in the world, there is war and tragedy.

It has been said, "peace is the brief, glorious moment in history when everybody stands around reloading." [55]

The word "peace" is used over 370 times in the Bible. Obviously, peace is important, or it would not have been used so many times. Today, we begin our time in Hebrews with an emphasis on this most elusive emotion.

Please read **Hebrews 12:14-29**.

This passage begins with an exhortation to "pursue peace with all people." I know what you are thinking.

"Really? *All people*? Surely not all people? This guy did not know the people I have to put up with. Pursue peace with them? Not gonna happen."

I, too, was hopeful for a little bit of leeway with this "all people" issue, but when I looked up the word "all," I found it had a very significant meaning. All means all, everyone. Hmm! No getting out of this one. The writer really meant that we are to try to have peace with everyone.

Now, our task is to figure out how to make that happen, but first we need to make sure we understand what peace really is.

The Greek word used for peace is *eirene*. Interestingly enough, while peace is a noun, I find that it is derived from a Greek verb (remember a verb is an action word) that means to join. When people join an organization or group, very often they do so because they have something in common or a common need.

Allow me to share the definition of peace with you from my *Zodhiates Key Word Study Bible* in an effort to build a basis for world peace.

"Peace, tranquility, repose, calm; harmony, accord; well-being prosperity. It denotes a state of untroubled, undisturbed, well-being." [56]

I don't know about you, but I want to get in line to sign up for that. Calgon, take me away! Calm, tranquility, undisturbed…yep, sounds like a bubble bath is in my future and yours, doesn't it? And while a bubble bath sounds divine, I hope to convince you that there is something much better that brings true and lasting peace, rather than peace that recedes as the bathwater cools and the bubbles pop.

Please turn to **Isaiah 9:6** and note what reference you find to peace in this verse.

_____

_____

_____

Now go to **John 14:27** and write out Jesus' words in the space below.

_____

_____

_____

Hundreds of years before the birth of Christ, Isaiah prophesied that He would be the Prince of Peace, the Ruler over peace. To affirm this prophecy, Jesus made it very clear He would be leaving His peace with them after He died, rose from the grave, and ascended back to heaven. It was His to give away to His followers.

Where does **John 10:30** infer that the peace Jesus left on earth ultimately comes from?

_____

_____

So, the peace Jesus gave His disciples when He left earth for heaven ultimately came from the Father. Jesus told us in John 14 that He only spoke words and did things ordained by the Father, so on this earth, Jesus joined in the work of the Father.

In **Acts 10:36** we are told what Jesus' job was while on this earth. Hint: look for the word peace.

_____

The preaching of peace that Jesus did while on this earth is referenced in **Ephesians 6:15**. What is it called in this passage that details our spiritual armor?

_____

The gospel of peace. Now, when you and I think of the word gospel, we associate it with the salvation message, don't we? Consider the remainder of the definition of _eirene_ or peace from Mr. Zodhiates:

> "Such a state of peace is the object of divine promise and is brought about by God's mercy, granting deliverance and freedom from all the distresses that are experienced as a result of sin. Hence the message of salvation is called the gospel of peace, for this peace can only be the result of reconciliation between man and God brought about by the atonement." [57]

Ahh, now we are getting somewhere. The message of salvation is called the gospel of peace and God, through Jesus Christ, is the author of peace. I hope I just proved that scripturally.

The ultimate purpose of the gospel of peace is salvation and the ultimate purpose of salvation is reconciliation or a bringing together in harmony. A good question to ask at this point would be: Who or what is being reconciled?

Let's turn to 2 Corinthians 5. I hope your heart takes this in and processes it because this lesson could be the very way whirled peas, um, no, world peace begins to break out all over the place.

Please read **2 Corinthians 5:17-21** and answer the following statements true or false:

T F : You can be a new creation outside of Christ.

T F : God reconciles us to Himself through Jesus.

T F : Once we are reconciled to God we have a job of sharing that reconciliation with others.

T F : People can be reconciled to God through meditation, Hinduism, Buddhism, or Islam.

The peace that Jesus left for believers is the salvation message: Jesus was born to die—to pay the price for my sin and yours. It is only when we accept the work of Jesus on the cross to cover our sin that we are reconciled, or made right, with God. Our hearts are joined with the heart of God, and at that moment, the peace of God is ours to claim and make our own.

The only way we can have true peace is to have Jesus as the ruler of our lives. True peace is what this world so desperately needs. All too often the peace seen by the world is a fake peace that lasts only until the drug wears off. The peace of God is not a drug-induced high that purports to cover whatever difficulty the person is enduring. No, the peace of God is a calmness and trust in God's power and purpose, no matter the situation.

Ok, now let's finish up this discussion of peace right back where we began in **Hebrews 12:14**.

What are we to pursue with all people?

_____

_____

_____

So, if we pursue peace with all people, what we are really doing is seeking to bring them to Christ, and this is exactly what the rest of verse 14 says when it includes holiness as something to pursue. The writer goes on to remind us that without peace and holiness not one person will see the Lord. Jesus made it clear that He was and is the only way to the Father, and it is our job to make Jesus known so others can come to know Him.

I would like to end this week of study by sharing with you a poem written by Francis of Assisi. I hope our discussion of peace today and the content of this beautiful poem will allow you to see your job as a minister of reconciliation in a whole new light.

Lord, make me an instrument of Your peace!

Where there is hatred, let me sow love;

Where there is injury, pardon;

Where there is doubt, faith;

Where there is despair, hope;

Where there is darkness, light;

Where there is sadness, joy.

Oh, Divine Master, grant that I may not so much seek

To be consoled, as to console;

To be understood, as to understand;

To be loved, as to love.

For it is in giving that we receive;

It is in pardoning that we are pardoned;

It is in dying that we are born to eternal life!

—St Francis of Assisi

MEDITATION MOMENT:

How is your peace today? If you know Jesus as Lord, then you have access to God's perfect peace. Are you appropriating His peace? Are you being a minister of reconciliation and sharing Jesus with other people? Spend some time praying about this matter of peace in your heart and life. God longs for you to know His peace.

May I Serve You?

This week's recipe comes from my friend, Kathryn Nelson, who is part of my Tuesday morning Bible study group. Kathryn shared with me that her son requests this coffee cake for his birthday each year. Now, I know why! It is a delectable mixture of fluffy cake, cinnamon sugar, and semi-sweet chocolate chips. Even for a girl who doesn't eat very much chocolate, this recipe is a hit. It is definitely one I will use over and over.

I think the perfect partner to this dessert would be a cup of Café Escapes® Dark Chocolate Hot Cocoa.

RECIPE

CHOCOLATE CHIP COFFEE CAKE

2 cups all purpose flour

1 ½ teaspoons baking powder

1 teaspoon baking soda

½ teaspoon salt

1 ¼ cup sugar, divided

1 teaspoon cinnamon

1 stick unsalted butter, at room temperature

2 large eggs, at room temperature

1 cup sour cream

1 teaspoon pure vanilla extract

1 cup chocolate chips
(I chose semi-sweet)

Preheat oven to 350 degrees. Grease an 8-inch square, baking pan. In a medium bowl, mix together the flour, baking powder, baking soda, and salt. In a small bowl, combine ¼ cup sugar and cinnamon. Using an electric mixer, beat together the butter and remaining 1 cup of sugar until fluffy, about 5 minutes. Beat in the eggs, one at a time. Beat in sour cream and vanilla. Fold in the flour mixture, in two parts, until just combined. Pour half the batter into the cake pan and sprinkle with half the cinnamon-sugar mixture and half the chocolate chips. Spoon the remaining batter as evenly as possible over the filling, spreading gently. Sprinkle with remaining cinnamon-sugar and chocolate chips.

Bake until golden and a toothpick inserted in the center comes out clean, approximately 30-35 minutes.

Week 8 – The Daily Brew – So, What?

Today, we begin the last week of our study of the book of Hebrews. I have learned so much about this marvelous book, and I've been encouraged to stay strong in my faith, even in the midst of difficulty. I hope you have too. Although most of us are not tempted to turn away from Jesus to other religions, we are sometimes significantly tempted to walk away because of the lure of the world. Satan knows what carrot to dangle in front of each generation and individual. For our generation, the carrot usually has something to do with money or earthly significance.

This week, we are going to be studying Hebrews chapter 13 and asking ourselves a very important question. If we were sitting across the table from each other with a piece of pecan pie and a cup of coffee I hope you would ask me this key question:

"So, what, Leah? How does all this studying of Hebrews change my world? Why is it important that I just spent seven weeks learning about the BETTER priest, the BETTER tabernacle, the BETTER covenant, and the BETTER sacrifice? What difference should it make to my life?"

You are so smart! I am glad you asked. If our time in the Word does not change us, we have not interacted with the Word in the way we should. As we learned in Hebrews 4:12, the Scriptures are living and active, but the Word cannot change our lives if we don't fully engage with it. So, what's the big deal about Hebrews? Give me five more days, and with the help of the writer of Hebrews, I will do my dead level best to answer those questions for you. Let's jump in, shall we?

Day 1 – Is Your Faith Showing?

If you have read my writing for any length of time, you have probably heard me confess my appalling lack of the spiritual gift of hospitality…*overnight* hospitality to be exact. I love having folks into my home for a meal or party, but I want them to GO HOME when it is time to go to bed. I think it is some sort of weird chromosomal abnormality. My home is my sanctuary, and I peg out (collapse from exhaustion) on the discomfort meter when I have overnight company.

Recently, I found a kindred spirit in my Bible study pal, Noelle. We were in our small group one day, and Noelle confessed that she does not like to have company in her home. She loves her family, as do I, but otherwise, she is totally uncomfortable with overnight, stay-a-long-time company. I nearly jumped up and shouted, "*I LOVE YOU, MY INHOSPITABLE SISTER!*" I'm not the only one. Whew! I was beginning to think I was totally abnormal.

At Christmas this past year, we received a picture of Noelle's family and a letter detailing what everyone in the family had been up to in 2012. At the end of the letter, the reader was invited, "Come visit us if you are in the area. We would love to have you."

Immediately, I picked up my mobile device and shot off a text to Noelle that said, "I KNOW you did not write your Christmas letter. I KNOW IT. You would never invite the world at large to come visit, nor would I."

She and I have laughed about it because, indeed, she did not write the letter. Her husband is the Christmas letter writer. Noelle and I definitely need a hospitality infusion!

Perhaps the writer of Hebrews knew a few people within his congregation that were afflicted with the same problem that Noelle and I have. After spending 12 chapters contrasting the Old Covenant with the New Covenant, the author abruptly turns his attention to daily life.

Please read the following verses in **Hebrews 13** and write a short synopsis of what each says:

Verse 1 –

_____

_____

_____

Verse 2 –

_____

_____

_____

Verse 3 –

_____

_____

_____

Verse 16 –

_____

_____

_____

Verse 17 –

_____

_____

_____

Here we find the author of Hebrews telling his congregation that their faith should produce some very clear patterns in their daily lives. (Ok, press the hold button, and let's make sure we are clear on one issue before we move on.) It is the old "faith versus works" dilemma. Well, it isn't really a dilemma unless you fail to understand how all of it works. Let's take a minute and review for the sake of clarity.

Paul, under the inspiration of the Holy Spirit, understood that there would be a bit of confusion about faith and works, so he addressed this in a couple of places. I want you to read as we look at the issue of works as an outgrowth of faith.

How does **Ephesians 2:8** tell us we have been saved?

_____

_____

_____

Ephesians 2:9 tells us that our salvation is NOT a result of what?

_____

_____

Paul words this same concept a bit differently in **Romans 3:20**. What does this verse tell us does not save or justify us before God?

_____

_____

Galatians 2:16 wraps this up in a nice, neat package. Please answer the following true or false:

T F :   Works of the law bring justification.

T F :   Salvation is by faith and works.

T F :   Faith in Jesus is the only way to obtain salvation.

We are saved by faith, and only by faith in Jesus Christ. It is because of God's grace that we are saved, and not because of anything you or I do. Nothing. *Nada*. You can serve yourself into oblivion in the church or on the mission field, but those works will never make you right before God. Only believing in Jesus as your Lord and Savior can justify or save you.

Grace offers salvation. Faith brings salvation. Works signal salvation. Understand? Now let's get back to Hebrews 13.

In the final chapter of Hebrews, we find the writer putting a P.S. on his message. It is almost as if he had wrapped up his sermon, and then decided to say one more thing. He begins by talking about how those who are Christians should show love to our Christian brothers and sisters, as well as to those who are not of the faith.

I can almost hear him in verse one when he urges the church to love each other with *phileo*, or brotherly love. Perhaps there had been some bickering in the church, and he felt like he needed to remind the members of the body of Christ that they would be known by the love they have for one another.

The way we treat our fellow humans shouts with a megaphone to an unbelieving world whether or not our faith has changed us. If we cannot even love those who are supposed to be of the same blood, Christ's blood, why would the unbelieving world want what we say we have? I wish it were not so, but all too often Christians are very quick to shoot down our brothers and sisters and very slow to come to their assistance. We must stop destroying our own.

Next, the writer encourages the church to show love to strangers and prisoners. In ancient times, Christians were very cautious about both of these groups. One never knew if a stranger was a spy sent to discover a Christian church and bring persecution to the believers. It was often dangerous to show hospitality to strangers, yet the writer called the church body to do just that. Likewise, to affiliate with prisoners could cause one to be viewed as a criminal, and perhaps be arrested. The Christian life should rarely be about what we get out of it, but rather what we can pour into other lives, no matter the risks.

In verse 16 the author acknowledges that what he is asking will be a sacrifice for many, and perhaps even a danger. The encouragement comes in knowing that God knows the circumstances and is pleased with such sacrifices.

Please write out **John 13:34-35** below.

_____

_____

_____

_____

Love for brothers and sisters in Christ. Love for strangers. Love for the imprisoned. Do good and share.

How are you doing on these? Our faith *must* make a difference in how we treat other people. If it doesn't, then it needs to be examined for genuineness. The lost world will know we are Christ's followers by the way we treat others. Our words, our actions, our passions, and our thoughts must all be informed by our faith in Jesus Christ. So, how well are you loving, sharing and doing good things for others?

MEDITATION MOMENT:

How *are* you doing in the area of loving others? Is your faith showing? Is your faith making a difference in you? Be honest with yourself and with God. Journal about it here.

Day 2 – I Do, Not I Don't

I had no intention of devoting an entire day of study to the topic of marriage. I do not consider myself to be an expert on the topic; however, as I began reviewing chapter 13 of Hebrews, it quickly became evident that the Lord was directing me to talk about marriage today. I've begged Him to let me off the hook with this one, but He doesn't seem inclined to do so. I considered throwing myself on the floor, crying loudly, and flailing around like a fish, but I know my God. He will just wait for me to finish my fit and then say, "Okay, now let's get on with the work." So, on I get.

The *New King James Version* states Hebrews 13:4 in this way: *Marriage is honorable among all, and the marriage bed undefiled; but fornicators and adulterers God will judge.*

I would submit to you that marriage has lost much of its honor in America and around the world today. Not because God has removed the honor, but because we have not acted with honor toward marriage. Consider some data from the US Census Bureau's website in 2009:

In 2008 approximately 2.2 million marriages took place. In the same year approximately 1 million people reported divorcing. This brings the divorce rate in the general population to almost 50% depending on which statistics you look at.

According to a Barna Group report released in 2008, 33% of Christians (evangelical and non-evangelical) have experienced at least one divorce. [58] The divorce rates climb higher for Christians and non-Christians when you consider subsequent marriages.

What about statistics on infidelity in marriage? These are very murky numbers because of the inaccuracy of reporting. While men are sometimes considered "studs" if they cheat, women are considered to be loose, or even worse; so it stands to reason that men might over-report marital infidelity, while women might under-report. *The General Social Survey (GSS)* conducted by University of Chicago researchers is the best data available for marital infidelity. The data have stayed the same for almost 40 years…approximately 10 percent of married folks admit to cheating on their spouse.

Then there is the data on sex and young people, which really doesn't cover the whole gamut of those having sex outside of or before marriage, but we have to start somewhere. *The Centers for Disease Control Youth Risk Surveillance – United*

States 2011 found that among US high school students (I'm going to say that is ages 14-18 years), 47.4% reported having ever had sex. [59]

Did you get that? Almost 50% of high school age children have had sex. 33.7% report having had sex in the previous 3 months and 15.3% report having had sex with four or more people during their short little lives.

No, friends, marriage is not considered to be honorable by a large portion of our population. We shake our heads at our children having sex before marriage, but so many parents are not doing any better—divorces, affairs, kids being raised by homosexual parents, and children being raised by parents who are not married but living together. It stands to reason that kids are only doing what they see the adults in our society do. Monkey see, monkey do.

Now, before someone who knows me writes me a letter proclaiming me to be a hypocrite, I'll go ahead and tell you that I have walked much of the road we are discussing. I am not pointing a finger at anyone without having three fingers point back at me. I made some poor, poor decisions earlier in my life. None of it was God's plan for me. All of it had painful consequences attached. I have deep regrets over it, but I also live today in the forgiveness and cleansing of Jesus Christ who, at my confession and repentance, wiped the slate clean for me. Praise His Merciful Name!!

So, how do we restore honor to marriage? That is the question on the table for today. How do we allow our faith in Jesus Christ to help us keep our marriage covenants and help us remain pure before marriage?

I believe there are three things we must do to begin to restore honor to marriage:

1.   Understand the importance of covenant

2.   Know there will be consequences and blessings attached to our choices

3.   Make up our minds to be pure

Let's look at each of these today.

Understand the importance of covenant

The issue of covenant is so much bigger and more important than most of us understand. There are several key covenants in the Bible such as the Noahic Covenant (Genesis 6), the Abrahamic Covenant (Genesis 15), the Davidic Covenant (2 Samuel 7), and the New Covenant (Jeremiah 31:31-34). Each of these covenants was initiated by God, and had blessings for obedience and curses for disobedience associated with them. The covenants were eternal and remain in effect today.

When we marry, we enter into a marriage covenant before God. Let's look at a few key verses pertaining to this topic.

Please write **Genesis 2:24** in the space below.

_____

_____

_____

_____

It is important for us to look at the Hebrew words used here to better grasp the enormity and permanence of the marriage relationship. There is a deliberate order of actions in this verse. There is a leaving, a joining, and a staying. The man leaves his parents, joins himself to his wife, and they are one flesh, hence they stay together. It is physically impossible for me to leave my flesh/body/skin behind. It goes where I go. It experiences everything I experience. When others see me, they see my flesh, or body. Other than through physical death, it is impossible to dissociate my flesh from my soul or spirit. This is how God designed the marriage covenant.

The Hebrew word used at the end of the verse for flesh is *basar* and it means "physical flesh, person, body, the physical skin." God's intent was, and still is, that when a man and woman marry, they become as if they were one person. Only death would break the marriage covenant between a man and a woman.

This is affirmed in Malachi 2:15 where God, speaking through Malachi, reminds Israel that two people who enter into a marriage covenant become one person. The breaking of the marriage covenant is a breaking of faith, according to Malachi 2:16. We will come back to that in a moment.

Jesus reiterated this in **Matthew 19:4-6**, quoting Genesis 2:24. He then went on to add an admonishment in verse 6 that we hear in almost every marriage ceremony.

What is that admonishment?

_____

_____

_____

Why do you think we treat this command and admonishment so lightly?

_____

_____

_____

_____

What God has joined together, let no man take apart. In our own pride and self-centeredness, we have decided this command is archaic and unnecessary. Our happiness, our comfort, our desires are more important to us than being obedient to God's command.

Please do not read more into this than I am saying. I am not saying that men or women who are being abused by their spouse should remain with that spouse. They need to remove themselves and their children from danger immediately. They need to get to a safe place, and then allow the Lord to deal with their spouse. God is still in the heart-changing business, if we will give Him the time and space to work.

Simply "falling out of love" with one's spouse, on the other hand, is not biblical grounds for breaking the marriage covenant. Only sexual immorality offers biblical grounds for divorce, and even then, remarriage is not allowed as long as the spouse lives. We have made marriage more about us than about being obedient to God.

Once again, I have walked this road. I did not make godly choices, and I've paid a price for it; however, for those who already have gone through divorce, I want you to know that this is not an unforgivable sin. God's willingness to forgive us for divorce, adultery, or any other sin is because of His grace. All we have to do is ask Him for forgiveness, from the depths of a repentant heart, and it is ours. A word of warning! We should not trample grace and think we can repeatedly marry and divorce to satisfy our happy-meter. Proffered grace should give us the motivation to make better, God-honoring choices concerning marriage in the future.

Know there will be consequences and blessings attached to our choices

Returning to Malachi 2, we are told a bit about this business of consequences and blessings related to marriage and divorce. God is speaking to the Israelite priests in this passage, but I believe we can apply this to ourselves since we have been called a royal priesthood for Christ's earthly kingdom. Let's take a look.

Please read **Malachi 2:13-16** and answer the following questions:

In **verse 13**, what is the evidence that the priests have displeased God?

_____

_____

Verse 14 tells us the reason why God has stopped regarding the offerings of the priests. What is it?

_____

_____

What terms are used to describe the wife in **verse 14**? NOTE: There are 2 descriptions.

_____

_____

Verse 15 tells us why God made a husband and wife one flesh (remember Genesis 2:24?). What is it?

_____

_____

What exceedingly strong words does God say about divorce in **verse 16**?

_____

_____

Why does God hate divorce according to **verse 16**?

_____

_____

_____

The priests had been unfaithful to their wives, and God was not a bit happy about it. He had ceased accepting their offerings because of their unfaithfulness to their wives.

I find the wording God uses in verse 16 to describe why he hates divorce very curious. He says divorce covers one's garment in violence. The Hebrew word used here for violence is *hamas*. Does that ring a bell with anyone? HINT: *Hamas*

is the Sunni Muslim Palestinian extremist (read that "terrorist") group based in the Gaza Strip in Israel. Violence is their calling card.

Consider the meaning of *hamas*: "to be violent, hurt. Violence oppression, wickedness, wrong, unrighteous gain. Signifies the violence that was one of the reasons God sent the flood. This word comes from a word that means to oppress, to be bold, be violent, treat violently, hurt, overthrow, tear down." [60]

If you have ever been through a divorce or are the child of divorced parents, you can likely understand the usage of this word in relation to divorce. It hurts those involved. It is a tearing down of something God intended to remain for eternity. Children of divorce are often used as weapons by one spouse against another. Words are exchanged that are hurtful—sometimes even violent. No one comes out of divorce unscathed. No one.

No doubt about it. Marriage can also be painful, but the promised blessings that come from being obedient and faithful to your marriage covenant are kept by God, and He will be faithful to keep them.

Make up our minds to be pure

Finally, we must make up our minds to remain pure and faithful to God and to our marriage covenants. Whether you are married or single, you must be intentional about guarding your purity. Only you can make that decision. Make up your mind ahead of time…before you get into a situation where you are forced to make a quick decision about remaining pure. If you have vowed before God to remain pure and faithful, it will be easier to stay true to that decision when temptations arise. The consequences of unfaithfulness to God are simply not worth whatever temporary pleasure one may experience. Trust me on this one. I know from experience.

MEDITATION MOMENT:

Friend, I'd like to think that everyone who does this Bible study has remained faithful to God sexually and honored marriage in his or her heart; however, I'm not naïve enough to think it is true…not in the day in which we live. So, what do I leave you with today? I leave you with God's grace, forgiveness, and fresh manna for a new day. Today is the day you get to start over—walking in forgiveness and grace if you have sinned sexually. If you have broken your marriage covenant, grace and forgiveness are yours for the asking. If you are considering dishonoring your marriage covenant, it is not too late to make a different, and hopefully, godly choice. Today, I offer you an audience with the One who loves you more than you can imagine. Spend some time opening your heart up to Him. You will find amazing love, grace, and forgiveness.

Day 3 – The Sin That Few Confess

"Lord, please forgive me for coveting."

My guess is that very few people utter these words publicly. Seriously, have you ever heard anyone ask forgiveness for coveting? I haven't. What's worse, rarely have I asked the Lord to forgive *me* for my acts of covetousness!

It isn't because I've never committed this sin. Most assuredly, I have. But confess it openly? Umm, NO! We confess adultery and alcoholism. We confess pride and pornography. We confess lying and larceny. So, why don't we confess our covetousness? Perhaps the answer lies in the fact that we really don't understand the meaning of the word, or how seriously God takes this business of coveting.

Today, our goal in Bible study is to delve into this topic and try to become more informed and humble about our need to address this sin.

Let's begin with our focal verses in **Hebrews 13:5-6**. Read these two verses and paraphrase them in the space below.

_____

_____

_____

With only a few exceptions, Hebrews 13:5 warns us against the love of money. The *New King James Version* words the verse this way: *Let your conduct be without covetousness; be content with such things as you have.*

I think we all know the caution offered in the Bible about the love of money, and how that love can be disastrous. Today, I want us to look at this word "covet" in a much broader sense than just with money, and we will use the NKJV wording as our springboard.

Approximately 30 times in the Scriptures, the word *covet* or a form of the word (i.e. covetous, covetousness, greed) is used. Greed! Ah, now there's a word we understand a bit better.

Let's look at a few of these instances and see if we can find a common theme running through the verses. Please look up the following Bible verses and note what it says about coveting. NOTE: the word *covet* will not be used in every verse. Look for related ideas.

Exodus 20:17

Proverbs 28:16

Jeremiah 22:17

Micah 2:2

Luke 12:15

1 Corinthians 6:9-10

_____

_____

_____

_____

Ephesians 5:3-5

_____

_____

_____

_____

There are two things I hope you discovered in these verses: coveting is not fitting for the saints of God (that's you and me, friend), and it is often associated with violence or oppression. Hold on to that. We will come back to it in just a moment.

Let's stop for a moment and consider the definition of _covet_ because I believe it will give us insight into the verses we just read.

In the Old Testament, the Hebrew word for covet is _hamad,_ and it means "to desire, covet, long for, to be desirable, be costly, be precious, to feel delight. It refers to an inordinate, ungoverned selfish desire." [61]

Let's focus on the portion of this definition that says, "refers to an inordinate, ungoverned selfish desire." But first, take a look at the New Testament Greek word used for _covet_ which adds a new dimension to our thinking.

The Greek word _epithymeo_ comes from two words, _epi_ which means "in" and _thymos_ meaning "passion." The definition goes on to tell us that this word means "to desire, long for, lust for. The word refers to the inclining of one's affections toward or setting of one's heart upon something. The force of the preposition _epi_ is directive, pointing to an object. Hence, it means to desire something in particular, want something specific, crave or lust for a certain thing, direct one's affection toward a definite object." [62]

If you will allow me to meld these two definitions for a moment, I think we will get a full picture of the importance of this word covet. Coveting is the inordinate, ungoverned selfish desire or longing for an object, position, or person.

I'm going one step further and adding the following to the definition: Coveting will often lead to violence or oppression, and is almost always associated with idolatry.

Let's consider these two issues of idolatry and violence as they relate to covetousness or greed. I don't think we will have too much trouble understanding this connection. When we long for or lust after something with an ungoverned desire, that thing or person becomes of prime importance to us. We think about it a lot. We actually elevate that thing or person in our minds and hearts, as the longing and desire to acquire it increases. The basic definition of idolatry is worshiping something or someone other than God. When we elevate the object of our desire to the point of coveting, we have fallen into idolatry.

What does **Exodus 20:4** say about idolatry?

_____

_____

_____

Right-o! Thou shalt not. Same words used in Exodus 20:17 about coveting. God said "no" to both.

What about the association between violence and coveting? Once again, I don't think it takes too much pondering to figure this out. We can use any one of several examples…money, drugs, sex, possessions, control. Once a person sets his or her heart on, and begins to lust after, an object or person, all too often he or she will go to extraordinary lengths to obtain the desired object. Anyone getting in the way could be in danger of violence or oppression. Now, most of us would not do bodily harm to another human being simply because we don't get what we want. At least, I hope we wouldn't! But, would we do harm to our heart and our relationship with God? Would we suppress, as it were, our Lord and His Holy Spirit in our desire to have what we think we want? Let me offer a personal example to further explain?

In 2007 God placed an unmistakable call to ministry on my life and heart. I answered the call, and He began to open doors of opportunity for me to speak and write. Over the years, I have had opportunities to speak to many wonderful women and girls at events all across the Southeast. In addition, God has blessed my writing ministry with the opportunity to write and publish two Bible studies, as well as sharing my heart through weekly and monthly devotionals on my blog and at other websites.

Occasionally, however, when ministry is quiet, I have been guilty of allowing my focus to drift. I see another speaker sharing at more events, or larger events, and I begin to desire to be in a different place in ministry than where God has me. I see an author being blessed with a publishing contract for her work, and I covet (oh yes, I said "covet") a publishing contract for *my* work. Although I know my ministry belongs to God, and all ministry has seasons of quiet, my "ungoverned, selfish desire" is for more and bigger and better for *me*. I resent the blessing that God has showered on another and covet it for myself. Soon, my eyes and heart have suppressed Jesus and elevated as an idol the thing or position I desire for myself.

Thankfully, it is not long before the Holy Spirit knocks gently on my head and gets my attention in a big way. It usually goes something like this:

> "For I know the plans I have for you, Leah. They are plans for you personally. They may not look like the plans I have for so-and-so. You need to take your eyes off of what I am doing in her life and redirect your gaze and your heart back to Jesus. Trust Him to give you the desires of your heart, if those desires line up with His desire for your life."

See how sneaky and oppressive covetousness is? You don't even realize that your heart has unseated Jesus from His rightful throne and put something or someone else in His place. Friend, I urge you to ask the Lord to help you be aware of this issue of coveting in your life. It can happen to anyone, and it may not always be about money, as you can see from my experience.

MEDITATION MOMENT:

One of the signs of true faith and spiritual maturity is being able to discern the leading and voice of the Holy Spirit when we sin. Have you ever heard the Holy Spirit calling you out on this issue of coveting? Are you currently coveting anything or anyone? If so, perhaps talking to the Lord about it will help you rid yourself of covetousness. Spend some time now journaling about this issue as it pertains to you personally.

Day 4 — By Faith, I Will Not Fear

Even a seasoned airline traveler can experience moments of fear in the air…or on the ground, for that matter. I love what Leonard Sweet says about air travel:

> Travel is hard enough without the airline industry scaring us with their terminology. As I drive to the airport, watching for signs that indicate what exits to take, I wonder what sadist named the place where you trust your all to a creaking bunch of nuts and bolts Terminal. When I check in at the counter, I remember, this particular flight was chosen by my travel agent for one reason—it was the cheapest available. When it's time to land, why does the flight attendant have to remind us that we are making our final approach? (On a recent flight, the attendant announced reassuringly, "We will be in the ground very shortly.") When the flight attendant warns us not to move until the plane has reached a complete stop, I wonder what an incomplete stop would be like. [63]

I am a seasoned airline traveler and rarely fear flying. I had never thought about any of the issues Sweet brings up, but you bet your life, I'll think about them from now on!

Fear. Obviously God knew it was something most humans would battle in the journey of life. It has been said there are over 360 verses in the Bible that deal with fear. Today, I want us to consider this issue of fear and learn how we can overcome it by faith.

I think it is great that the writer of Hebrews addressed the issue of fear for his readers. Recall that the Hebrew Christians were experiencing persecution as a result of their faith in Christ. Their pastor, the author of Hebrews, wanted to reassure them that fear was unnecessary. Two thousand plus years later, he offers that same reassurance to you and me.

Please read **Hebrews 13:6-9**.

In the space below please write out verses 6 and 8 in their entirety from a translation of your choice.

_____

_____

_____

_____

_____

What I hope to convince you of today is that because Jesus Christ is the same yesterday, today, and forever, there is no need to fear.

Pastor and author Charles Swindoll tells a story that we will use as the launch pad for our study today.

> One evening Swindoll and his wife were keeping a couple of their grandchildren, and as grandparents do, they had allowed the children to stay up much later than their regular bedtime. Suddenly, there was a knock at the door and one of the children grabbed Swindoll's arm, obviously frightened. Swindoll reassured the child that everything was okay, but the boy was not convinced, since the person at the door had knocked rather than used the doorbell.
>
> Swindoll went to the door and opened it to find a friend of one of his sons, who had dropped by unexpectedly. After the friend left, the grandchild was still holding onto Swindoll's leg, but seemed a bit less frightened. The boy looked at Swindoll and said, "Bubba, we don't have anything to worry about, do we?"
>
> Swindoll reassured the child, "No, we don't have anything to worry about. Everything is fine."
>
> Charles Swindoll went on to say the following: "You know why he was strong? Because he was hanging on to protection. As long as he was clinging to grandfather's leg, he didn't have to worry about a thing." [64]

So it is with you and me. As long as we hang on to the Lord, we don't have to fear. Did you get that? We don't HAVE to fear. We may choose to fear, but it is not necessary.

Let's pause and make one thing clear. I am not saying there will never be reason to fear. I am not saying bad things will not happen. I am not even saying that fear will never come calling. We live in a fallen world. There will probably be reason to be fearful. There will likely be bad things that will happen. Fear will come calling. How do I know?

Read Jesus' words in **John 16:33 (NIV1984)** and fill in the blanks. *I have told you these things, so that in me you may have _____. In this world you will _____ _____. But take heart! I have _____ the world*.

205

Jesus says we should have peace—the absence of fear and anxiety—because He has overcome the world. How has He overcome the world? Jesus has overcome the world by living as the God-man on earth, experiencing every trial and test that you and I experience, yet remaining sinless throughout His time on earth. His death on the cross, as payment for our sin and rebellion, defeated the stronghold of death for you and me. Every believer in Jesus Christ has this same overcoming ability through the indwelling Holy Spirit of God.

Paul knew this and was able to live in victory over fear. Let's allow Paul to speak words of encouragement into our hearts. Turn to **Romans 8** and answer the following questions:

Verse 28 tells us that God works for the good of whom?

_____

_____

In **verse 31** we are reminded that no one can be against us if who is for us?

_____

_____

Paul asks a rhetorical question in the first sentence of **verse 35**. What is it?

_____

_____

_____

How does **verse 37** describe you and me?

_____

_____

_____

List the things from **verses 38 and 39** that Paul was convinced would never separate us from the love of God in Jesus Christ.

_____

_____

_____

Think about it. That is an all-encompassing list if I've ever seen one.

Life cannot separate us from God's love.

Death cannot separate us from God's love.

Angels cannot separate us from God's love.

Demons cannot separate us from God's love.

The present cannot separate us from God's love.

The future cannot separate us from God's love.

No powers can separate us from God's love.

Height cannot separate us from God's love.

Depths cannot separate us from God's love.

Anything else in all creation cannot separate us from God's love.

I believe that list covers pretty much everything…except one thing. The only way you and I can be separated from God's love is if we willingly walk away from Him. Oh, His love will remain, you can be sure of that. God will not force His love on us. You and I must choose to remain attached to and plugged into His love.

How do we do that? We get to know Him through His Word. Time spent studying Scripture is never wasted time. Never. As you learn about God and His character, you begin to trust Him more. The more you trust God, the less you fear.

I know, I know. It sounds trite and very much like a formula, but it really works. I can't explain it. I just know it works. The better I know my Jesus through studying the Scriptures the more I trust Him to take care of me. The more I trust Him to take care of me, the less I fear. This doesn't happen overnight, nor is it the result of some weird incantation. It takes time, and it takes focus on God's Word.

Let's finish up today by taking a glance at the benefits of hanging on tightly to God and trusting the Lord in all things. Please turn to **Psalm 112** and read it through in its entirety. It is only 10 verses.

Now go back to each verse and list the benefits of trusting in the Lord. Don't rush through this. Allow Jesus to encourage your heart and deepen your trust in Him through this exercise. If one of the benefits resonates with you and your life circumstances, take a moment to journal a bit about it in the Meditation Moments section.

Verse 1 –

Verse 2 –

Verse 3 –

Verse 4 –

Verse 5 –

Verse 6 –

Verse 7 –

_____

_____

_____

Verse 8 –

_____

_____

_____

_____

Verse 9 –

_____

_____

_____

_____

Verse 10

_____

_____

_____

_____

MEDITATION MOMENT:

Great work today! How does this walk through Psalm 112 encourage you to trust the Lord in all things? How does it help you to have less fear?

_____

_____

_____

_____

_____

_____

Day 5 – Praise – The Proper Response

Week 8, Day 5—the final lesson in our Hebrews journey together. From this point, we walk on separately, but we walk on in faith. The beauty of the Christ-life is that you don't need me to walk on with you. All you need is Jesus, and I pray that I have shown Him to you in new portraits over the course of the past eight weeks. I've sought to show you Jesus, the BETTER sacrifice and Jesus, the BETTER priest. Both portraits are so crucial to living under the BETTER covenant, and ultimately living in the BETTER tabernacle one day in heaven.

I pray the words in this workbook have been God's words, and not my own. My hope is that you have come to love Jesus a little more than you did before you opened the pages of this study. Not because of my words, but because of the living and active Word of God. If you have a closer walk with Christ because of your time in this study, then I have done my job, and I raise my hands in praise to the One who called me to this task, Jehovah.

Praise. It is our focus as we turn the final pages of this study, and rightly so. It is the only appropriate response for what Jesus has done for us and in us. If I could sing (I cannot), I would burst forth in songs of praise to my Jesus. I might sing:

> "Praise Him, praise Him, Jesus our blessed Redeemer. For our sin He suffered and bled and died. He our Rock, our hope of eternal salvation. Hail Him! Hail Him! Jesus the crucified!" (Fanny Crosby, 1869.)

Or perhaps I would sing this:

> "Majesty, worship His majesty. Unto Jesus be all glory, honor and praise. So exalt, lift up on high, the name of Jesus. Magnify, come glorify, Christ Jesus the King. Majesty, worship His majesty. Jesus who died, now glorified, King of all Kings." (Jack Hayford, 1977)

Chances are really good that I might sing this grand old hymn:

> "Amazing grace, how sweet the sound, that saved a wretch like me. I once was lost, but now am found, was blind, but now I see." (John Newton, 1779)

Don't get me wrong, I love new contemporary praise and worship songs, but something about the older songs just blesses my heart in wonderful ways. The song choice is less important than the heart attitude from which it springs forth—an attitude of praise and thanksgiving for what Jesus has done for me. Me! A woman who made so many poor choices in her teens and twenties that grace seemed like a ridiculous thing to even hope for. Yet, God's amazing grace was applied to my sin, and they were washed clean.

Today, let's ponder the reasons we have discovered in the book of Hebrews to praise our Jesus.

Please read **Hebrews 13:10-25**. Now write out, in its entirety, the verse from this passage that speaks of praise. HINT: Check out verse 15.

_____

_____

_____

In verse 15 we see the writer of Hebrews giving his congregation a final encouragement to offer praise to Jesus for His work on earth and in heaven. He knew that offering praise would necessitate a sacrifice from the Hebrew Christians because of their circumstances of persecution, yet he urged them to offer it anyway. Sacrifices were such a key part of Judaism, and this wording ("sacrifice of praise") would have elicited deep emotion within the Hebrew Christians. The writer was telling them to offer a sacrifice of praise from their lips for the sacrifice made by Jesus.

Thus, he speaks to us as well. I can think of several reasons, based on our study of Hebrews, to offer praise today:

- *Jesus gave His life to be the ultimate Sacrifice for our sin.*

- *Jesus accepts us as we are, if we are willing to accept Him as our Savior.*

- *Jesus sits at the right hand of the Father and intercedes for us as our Priest.*

- *Jesus administers a New Covenant written on the fabric of our hearts, rather than on stone tablets.*

- *Jesus' death opened the way into the Holy of Holies, so you and I can approach God any time we desire.*

- *Jesus' resurrection made it possible for you and me to live eternally in heaven, the BETTER tabernacle, with God.*

- *When Jesus ascended to heaven, God sent the Holy Spirit to live in each of us and enable us to live the Christ-life on the dusty sod of earth.*

I feel the Lord encouraging me to place our Meditation Moment right smack in the middle of our lesson.

MEDITATION MOMENT:

Choose a reason to offer praise to Jesus this moment, and write a prayer of praise to Him in the space below. You may choose one of the reasons I have listed above, or you may have your own reason to praise Him. I would like to offer my own as a seed for you to begin.

> Jesus, the Name above all names. The One who looked down through the ages at me and saw my deep need for a fresh start and a new heart. Jesus. The name that is so sweet to me. I praise You because You love me just as I am. I worship You because Your holiness did not prevent You from laying aside Your God-ness and taking the form of a man who would ultimately die on the cross for me. For me! It slays me when I think of what You did for me. You left heaven, and all the wonders of that place where God dwells, to come to earth. You were born to die, and die You did—a horrendous death on the cross. Yet, the truly horrible part of it was that You became my sin. The perfect, holy, spotless Lamb of God took on every gross sin I would ever commit and gave me Your holiness and cleanness. Oh, the absurdity of it all. The wonder of it. I praise You, Jesus! I thank You! May I never get over it.

Now, it is your turn. Take all the time you need.

I hope you, like me, are wiping away tears of thanksgiving and praise. Let's complete our journey together by using some of the psalms as a springboard for our own praise. The book of Psalms is a magnificent place to go if you want to praise our God. I am offering you several references for portions of praise psalms. Use them to offer prayers of praise from your own lips. Yes, indeed, I want you to voice these praises aloud to the Lord, just as the writer of Hebrews asked his congregation to do. I am including space below so you can write them out if you would like, but it is important that you speak them aloud. Please choose at least two of the Scriptures below. Ready? Go!

Psalm 30:4-5

Psalm 34:1-4

Psalm 68:19-20

Psalm 84:10-11

Psalm 103:1-5

Psalm 106:1

Psalm 116:1-2

I hope you were blessed by that exercise. I think we spend most of our prayer lives in the asking mode and far too little in the praising mode. I know I'm guilty.

Friend, thank you for taking this journey through the book of Hebrews with me. God esteems your hard work and your heart for His Word. I esteem you and am so thankful you allowed me to be your guide through Hebrews. It has been my honor to serve you. And so, until we meet either here on this earth or in heaven above, I pray **Hebrews 13:20-21 (NLT)** over you:

Now may the God of peace—
who brought up from the dead our Lord Jesus,
the great Shepherd of the sheep,
and ratified an eternal covenant with his blood—
may he equip you with all you need
for doing his will.
May he produce in you,
through the power of Jesus Christ,
every good thing that is pleasing to him.
All glory to him forever and ever! Amen. [97]

May God's grace be with you all. Amen

END NOTES

1   Warren Wiersbe. *Be Confident: Live by Faith, Not by Sight* (Colorado Springs: David C Cook 2004), 5.

2   William L. Lane. *Word Biblical Commentary 47 A & B – Hebrews* (Nashville: Thomas Nelson Inc., 1991), xlvii.

3   Personal communication via The Point Ministries Blog, January 3, 2012, comments section.

4   John MacArthur. *MacArthur New Testament Commentary – Hebrews.* (Chicago: Moody 1983), 127.

5   Spiros Zodhiates. *Hebrew-Greek Key Word Study Bible - NIV.* (Chattanooga AMG Publishers, 2009), 1672.

6   William L. Lane. *Word Biblical Commentary 47 A & B - Hebrews.* (Nashville: Thomas Nelson, 1991), 85.

7   *Merriam Webster's Collegiate Dictionary – Eleventh Edition.* (Springfield: Merriam Webster, Inc. 2009), 1062.

8   Spiros Zodhiates. *Hebrew-Greek Key Word Study Bible - NIV.* (Chattanooga: AMG Publishers, 2009), 1629.

9   Lifeway Online Study Bible, KJV with Strongs. Lifeway.com.

10   Ibid

11   www.biblestudytools.com website

12   Lifeway Online Study Bible, KJV with Strong's. www.lifeway.com

13   Zodhiates, Spiros. *Hebrew-Greek Key Word Study Bible*, 1621.

14   Personal communication

15   Dr. Donnie Barnes. Barnes Bible Charts – Diagram of the Temple. Used by permission.

16   Reprinted by permission. *Word Biblical Commentary 47 A & B - Hebrews.* Lane, William L. 1991. Thomas Nelson Inc. Nashville, Tennessee. All rights reserved, 165.

17   Ibid., 166.

18   Ibid., 166.

19   Zodhiates, Spiros. *Hebrew-Greek Key Word Study Bible*, 1679.

20   Encarta Dictionary Online

21   Dr. Donnie Barnes. Barnes Bible Charts – Diagram of the Temple. Used by permission.

22   Zodhiates, Spiros. *Hebrew-Greek Key Word Study Bible*, 1612.

23   Ibid., 1508.

24   Ibid., 1524.

25   Ibid., 1508.

26   Reprinted by permission. *Word Biblical Commentary 47 A & B - Hebrews.*

Lane, William L. 1991. Thomas Nelson Inc. Nashville, Tennessee. All rights reserved, 209.

27 Used by permission. Excerpt taken from *Up With Worship* by Anne Ortlund. C 2005. B&H Publishing Group.

28 Merriam Websters Collegiate Dictionary – Eleventh Edition.

29 Copyright 2004. Warren Wiersbe. *Be Confident: Live by Faith, Not by Sight* published by David C Cook. Publisher permission required to reproduce. All rights reserved, 113.

30 Zodhiates, Spiros. *Hebrew-Greek Key Word Study Bible*, 1660.

31 Eliot, Elizabeth. *In the Shadow of the Almighty*. Harper and Row, 1958, 108

32 Denison, James. www.denisonforum.org. Online Essay from 2/5/12 entitled "Seven Plays that Changed the Super Bowl."

33 Ibid.

34 Taken from *Come Before Winter* by Charles R Swindoll. Copyright© 1985 by Tyndale House Publishers, Inc. Wheaton, Illinois. Used by permission of Tyndale House Publishers, Inc. All rights reserved, 365.

35 Moore, Beth. "Esther: It's Tough Being a Woman" Video. Lifeway Publishers: Nashville, Tennessee.

36 Copyright 2004. Warren Wiersbe. *Be Confident: Live by Faith, Not by Sight* published by David C Cook. Publisher permission required to reproduce. All rights reserved, 120-121.

37 MacArthur, John. *MacArthur New Testament Commentary – Hebrews*. Moody Publishers, Chicago, Ill. 1983, 299.

38 Ibid, 301.

39 Ibid, 332.

40 National Institute of Mental Health website.

41 Boice, James Montgomery. *Nehemiah: An Expositional Commentary*. Baker Books: Grand Rapids, Michigan 2005.

42 Pink, Arthur W. *Exposition of Hebrews*. Baker Books: Grand Rapids, MI. 1968.

43 Copyright 2004. Warren Wiersbe. *Be Confident: Live by Faith, Not by Sight* published by David C Cook. Publisher permission required to reproduce. All rights reserved, 60.

44 Reprinted by permission. *Word Biblical Commentary 47 A & B - Hebrews*. Lane, William L. 1991. Thomas Nelson Inc. Nashville. All rights reserved, 135.

45 Ibid, 145.

46 MacArthur, John. *MacArthur New Testament Commentary – Hebrews*. (Chicago: Moody Publishers) 1983, 129.

47 Ibid, 132.

48 Copyright 2004. Warren Wiersbe. *Be Confident: Live by Faith, Not by Sight* published by David C Cook. Publisher permission required to reproduce. All rights reserved, 63.

49 MacArthur, John. *MacArthur New Testament Commentary – Hebrews*. Moody Publishers, Chicago, Ill. 1983, 141.

50 *The Expositor's Bible Commentary—Abridged Edition: New Testament*. Zondervan: Grand Rapids, Michigan. 1994, 964.

51 Copyright 2004. Warren Wiersbe. *Be Confident: Live by Faith, Not by Sight* published by David C Cook. Publisher permission required to reproduce. All rights reserved, 64.

52 Ibid., 65-66.

53 MacArthur, John. *MacArthur New Testament Commentary – Hebrews*. Moody Publishers, Chicago, Ill. 1983, 146.

54 *The Expositor's Bible Commentary—Abridged Edition: New Testament*, 965.

55 Copyright 1977 Lloyd Cory. *Quote Unquote* published by David C Cook. Publisher permission required to reproduce. All rights reserved.

56 Zodhiates, Spiros. *Hebrew-Greek Key Word Study Bible*, 1615.

57 Ibid.

58 The Barna Group, Ltd. www.barna.org. *New Marriage and Divorce Statistics Released*. March 31, 2008.

59 www.publicdata.norc.org. General Social Survey. 1972-2006. Variable: evstray

60 "Youth Risk Behavior Surveillance" – United States, 2011. www.cdc.gov/mmwr/pdf/ss/ss6104.pdf.

61 Zodhiates, Spiros. *Hebrew-Greek Key Word Study Bible*, 1516.

62 Ibid, 1625.

63 Rowell, Edward K. *1001 Quotes, Illustration, and Humorous Stories for Preachers, Teachers, and Writers*. Baker Books: Grand Rapids, Michigan. 2008, 384-385.

64 Reprinted by permission. *Swindoll's Ultimate Book of Illustrations and Quotes*, Swindoll, Charles R, 2003, Thomas Nelson, Inc. Nashville, Tennessee. All rights reserved.